LONDON
A Visitor's Guide

LONDON

A Visitor's Guide

DAVID & CHARLES
Newton Abbot   London

Other useful books:
Bailey, Conrad. *Famous London Graves* (George Harrap & Co Ltd, 1976)
Benn's Blue Guide to London (Ernest Benn Ltd, 1975)
Delderfield, Eric R. *King's and Queens of England and Great Britain* (David & Charles, 7th impression 1979)
Gibson, Peter. *The Capital Companion* (Webb & Bower, 1985)
Hall, Martin. *Blue Plaque Guide to London* (Queen Anne Press, 1980)
Hellicar, Eileen. *Prime Ministers of Britain* (David & Charles, 1978)
Piper, David. *Companion Guide to London* (Collins, 1977)
Scott, Carolyn. *Westminster Abbey, Its Links with the Famous* (Sheldon Press, 1976)
Wickham, D. E. *Discovering Kings and Queens* (Shire Publications, 1980)
Winks, Robin W. *An American's Guide to Britain* (Charles Scribner's Sons, NY, 1977)
Yurdan, Marilyn, *Tracing Your Ancestors* (David & Charles, 1988)

All the photographs on the cover and inside the book are the copyright of The British Tourist Authority, unless stated otherwise.
(page 1) *Tower Bridge* (Woodmansterne Limited Watford)
(pages 2 & 3) *Houses of Parliament*

British Library Cataloguing in Publication Data

Dixey, Godfrey.
    London: a visitor's guide.
    1. London. Visitor's guides.
    I. Title
    914.21'04858

    ISBN 0-7153-9360-X

Typeset by Typesetters (Birmingham) Limited
and printed in West Germany
by Mohndruck GmbH
for David & Charles Publishers plc
Brunel House   Newton Abbot   Devon

Contents

Introduction

The idea for this little book came from working for several years at Westminster Abbey as a marshal, in which capacity I was in daily contact with many thousands of visitors. During this time I was constantly plied with questions, not only about the history of the abbey, but about British history in general.

Most of the questions, as might have been expected, came from North Americans, many of whom expressed a very great interest in history, and it is mostly for them that this book has been written. It is not intended to replace the many excellent and detailed guide books, nor to give any more than a very brief outline of the more important historical details. Rather it is meant as a framework for the more detailed information provided by guides and guide books.

I have also included a list of burial places of the kings and queens and other famous people, as well as a few tips and other pieces of information which may be useful to those visiting this country for the first time.

The Statue of Eros, Piccadilly (Woodmansterne Limited Watford)

1

London and its History

London has a population of about 7 million, divided into the City of London – a small area of about a square mile (2.6km^2), the financial centre of Britain – and thirty-two boroughs. It is the City to which I refer in the following brief history.

The origin of the name London is unknown, although it goes back to Celtic times. It was probably the site of a ford over the river. The importance of the City started in Roman times, when the name was latinised into Londonium. The Roman historian, Tacitus, described it as 'a busy emporium for trade and traders', and under the Romans it became an important administrative centre and the hub of their road system.

After the departure of the Roman legions, London formed part of the kingdom of the East Saxons until taken by the Danes.

The Guildhall

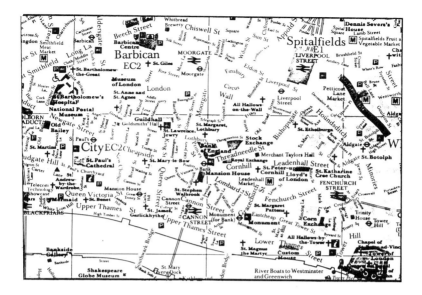

The City of London – the financial centre of Britain

In 886, King Alfred recovered London from the Danes, and reconstituted it under his son-in-law. When, later, the Danes conquered Britain, King Canute levied a sum of £10,500 on the City, one-eighth of the contribution of the whole of the country.

In 1067, William the Conqueror granted the City a charter, which is still preserved, establishing its citizens in the rights and privileges they had hitherto enjoyed. And it was the Conqueror who built the Tower of London.

The mayoralty was established in 1191, the first mayor being Henry Fitz Ailwyn, who held office for twenty-one years. A new charter was granted by King John in 1215, directing the mayor to be chosen annually, which has ever since been done, though in early times the same man held office more than once – the best known instance being Sir Richard Whittington, four times Lord Mayor, a title which was first used in 1414.

The Lord Mayor is chosen from two Aldermen who have served the office of Sheriff – a Saxon name for the King's representative in a shire with judicial and executive powers. The title of alderman dates back to Saxon times. There are twenty-five, representing various City Wards. The Lord Mayor is presented to the Lord Chief Justice at the Royal Courts of Justice on the second Saturday in November to make the final declaration of office, having been sworn in at the Guildhall on the previous day.

The procession to the Courts from the Guildhall is popularly known as the Lord Mayor's Show and is a free spectacle enjoyed by many thousands of spectators. Lord Mayors come from the ninety-seven City Guilds or Livery Companies, who derive their name from the distinctive dress, or livery, worn by their members in the fourteenth century. Each guild was originally confined to a particular trade such as mercers, grocers, drapers etc.

The City continued to grow in size and importance until, in 1665, it was devastated by the Great Plague which claimed some 90,000 victims and, a year later, by the Great Fire which, lasting 5 days, destroyed four-fifths of the City – 13,200 houses and 89 churches. Sir Christopher Wren, the architect and mathematician, put forward, in vain, an ambitious plan to reconstruct the City according to modern principles, but he was allowed to rebuild St Paul's Cathedral and many other churches.

Under Charles I, the City's privileges had been curtailed, but were reinstated under James II.

The first Census of London, in 1801, showed a population of 860,035 inhabitants. London suffered attacks from the air in World War I, mostly by Zeppelin airships, and 670 people were killed and 2,000 wounded; but the casualties and damage during Hitler's 'Blitz' in World War II were much more serious, with about 30,000 people killed. Much of the damage and casualties occurred in the City and the dockland area in the East End. Most of the war damage has now been repaired, though one can still see some reminders of the Blitz, especially ruined churches.

While the City remained as the hub of Britain, London was expanding westwards and, before the Conquest, Edward the Confessor had built the Palace of Westminster and Westminster Abbey. Other monarchs were responsible for more expansion and, gradually, except for the Royal Parks, the land was built over, particularly in Georgian and Victorian times, slowly spreading out as suburbs.

All these facets of the capital's history can be found in the sites and monuments described in the following pages.

The Tower of London

A State Procession

Marble Arch

2

Churches and Cathedrals

Westminster Abbey

The official name is the Collegiate Church of St Peter at Westminster. It is, and has been since 1066, the crowning place of monarchs, and was formerly a burial place of kings and queens.

In the eighth century, a Benedictine Abbey dedicated to St Peter was founded upon the present site, and given the name of West Minster, or 'western monastery'. This was rebuilt on a larger scale by Edward the Confessor, and consecrated in 1065. After the Norman Conquest, William I was crowned in front of the high altar, a procedure followed by every succeeding monarch except Edward V who was one of the princes murdered in the Tower of London, and Edward VIII who abdicated.

In 1245 Henry III, who greatly admired Edward the Confessor, decided to honour him by building a magnificent church in the French style of architecture. This new building, which consisted of the present choir, part of the nave, sanctuary, transept and shrine of the Confessor, with a Lady Chapel at the east end, was completed and consecrated in 1269.

After this rapid construction, the next stage, the rebuilding of the remainder of the nave, took a considerable period of time, 1376–1528. This period also included the Chantry Chapel of Henry V, and Henry VII's Chapel, the latter replacing Henry III's Lady Chapel. Henry VII's Chapel, originally intended to house the remains of Henry VI, is famous for the magnificent fan-vaulted ceiling with hanging pendants. Completed between 1503 and 1519, it is now the chapel of the Order of The Bath.

The final additions were the western towers, erected between 1732 and 1745. The church is 511ft (156m) in length, 200ft (61m) wide across the transepts, the lantern is 151ft (46m) high and the nave 101ft (31m). The exterior was restored between 1697 and 1720, also between 1875 and 1884, and is presently undergoing extensive reconstruction and repair.

The abbey escaped serious damage during World War II, although the roof of the lantern was burned down by incendiary bombs, and some of the windows were blown out. More serious damage to the windows, and to much of the interior decoration, had been caused by the Puritans.

Westminster Abbey ceased to be an abbey under the charge of an abbot in 1540 when the Benedictine abbot, Boston, surrendered it to the Crown. In the same year, Henry VIII made Westminster into a cathedral church with a bishop and dean. The Benedictine monastery was restored by Mary I in 1556, but it again ceased to be an abbey when Elizabeth I came to the throne. The Foundation Charter of the present Collegiate, exempt from the Archbishop of Canterbury and the Bishop of London, dates from 1560. It is known as a 'Royal Peculiar', the head of which is the Dean, whose appointment and authority derive from the Crown.

There are reputed to be approximately 3,000 people buried in the church or cloisters, including seventeen monarchs and many other famous men and women. There are many historic points of interest, such as the Coronation Chair and the Stone of Scone, Poets' Corner and the Chapter House.

The Stone of Scone, a stone upon which many of the early kings of Scotland had been crowned, was seized by Edward I in 1296 and placed in the care of the Abbot of Westminster. In 1298, Edward ordered a chair to be made to hold the Stone. The first sovereign to be crowned on the chair was his son, Edward II, and since then it has been used at all subsequent coronations. The Stone was removed by Scottish Nationalists in 1952, but returned in time for the coronation of our present queen in 1953.

Among the royal weddings which have taken place in the abbey are those of Queen Elizabeth and Prince Philip, George V and Queen Mary, George VI and Queen Elizabeth (the present queen's father and mother), Princess Margaret and Princess Anne, but not that of Prince Charles and Princess Diana, who were married in St Paul's Cathedral.

Although the abbey may be regarded as a museum and a repository of British history, it is still a living House of God, in which prayers are offered frequently and services held daily. Closely connected with the abbey is the adjoining Westminster School, founded by Elizabeth I in 1560, and now one of Britain's great public schools.

Next door to the abbey is the attractive church of **St Margaret, Westminster,** completed in 1523 and noted for its east window. Since 1621, St Margaret's has been the parish church of the House of Commons, and the scene of many fashionable weddings, including that of Winston Churchill.

(page 14) *Westminster Abbey*

(page 15) *St Paul's Cathedral*

St Paul's Cathedral

London's other great church is St Paul's Cathedral, Sir Christopher Wren's masterpiece. From about AD 600, there has always been a place of Christian worship upon this site at the top of Ludgate Hill, the first church being a wooden edifice endowed by King Ethelbert of Kent. This was burned down and rebuilt in stone between 675 and 685, laid waste by the Vikings, rebuilt again in 962, and again destroyed by fire in 1087. A larger church was then started and completed in 1220. Some 400 years later, Inigo Jones was asked to restore it, but the Civil War intervened and, in 1666, the church was completely destroyed in the Great Fire of London.

After several plans for the rebuilding had been put forward, the third plan of Wren's was accepted and, in 1675, work was started on the building which stands today. After many difficulties it was completed in 1708. The building follows the Renaissance style, and is dominated by the famous dome which is 122ft (37m) in diameter and 365ft (111m) high. Internally, the cathedral is 479ft (145m) long and 227ft (69m) wide at the transepts. The nave is 125ft (38m) across and 92ft (28m) high, and the total area of the cathedral is 87,400sq ft (8,021m^2).

Just before World War II the dome, around which runs the Whispering Gallery, was strengthened at the foundations and encircled by a steel chain. This may well have saved the dome from collapse when the cathedral was damaged by bombs during the war.

Many famous people are buried at St Paul's, and in the crypt are the tombs, among others, of Lord Nelson and the Duke of Wellington. St Paul's also contains the chapels of the Order of St Michael and St George and of the Order of the British Empire.

The cathedral is the headquarters of the Bishop of London, and was the scene of the wedding of Prince Charles and Lady Diana Spencer. Services are held daily, with prayers being offered hourly.

Southwark Cathedral

This is one of the two other cathedrals in London, Westminster being the third. Southwark stands in Borough High Street, south of the River Thames, and was developed from a Norman priory into the parish church of St Saviour (1540). After Westminster Abbey, it is London's finest Gothic church, dating from 1206. The nave collapsed and was rebuilt in 1838. Much was restored after damage in World War II.

Rich in monuments, it has many associations with William Shakespeare and the Bankside Players, and there is also a memorial and chapel dedicated to John Harvard, the founder of Harvard University, who was born nearby.

Southwark is the mother church of the Diocese of Southwark, which includes most of south London and was created in 1905.

Westminster Cathedral

Westminster Cathedral is the most important Roman Catholic church in England, the seat of the Archbishop of Westminster, head of the Roman Church in England and Wales.

Started in 1895, it was consecrated in 1910. It is a vast edifice, built in Byzantine style and dominated by a 284ft (86m) high campanile, or bell tower. The cathedral is 342ft (104m) long and the nave is the widest in England, 149ft (45m) (including the side chapels).

Central Synagogue

Situated in Great Portland Street, W1, this is considered to be one of the leading synagogues in Britain.

Central London Mosque

Situated in Park Road, NW8, on the edge of Regent's Park, this mosque was built in the 1970s.

OTHER CHURCHES

London contains many other churches of beauty and interest, even though a number were destroyed during the war. Among them are the following:

All Hallows, Barking-by-the Tower: Founded in 675, this has been much restored. It is now the guild church of Toc H, and contains a memorial to the dead of World War I and a very fine collection of brasses. William Penn was baptised here, and here John Quincy Adams, President of the United States, was married.

Brompton Oratory: Opened in 1884, near the museums in South Kensington, this is one of the most popular Roman Catholic churches in London.

Christ Church, Spitalfields: This was built 1723–9 in Baroque style by Wren's pupil, Nicholas Hawksmoor – the biggest of his churches.

(above) St Clement Danes; *(right)* St Martin-in-the-Fields, Trafalgar Square

St Andrew, Holborn: One of the largest of Wren's sixty-odd parish churches, it was restored after heavy bomb damage in World War II.

St Bartholomew-the-Great, Smithfield: The oldest church building in London, dating from Norman times. It has the capital's oldest medieval font and contains the tomb of Rahere, who founded St Bartholomew's Hospital.

St Bride, Fleet Street: Another Wren church which has been heavily restored after bomb damage. It was built on the site of a sixth-century stone church which lasted until the Great Fire of 1666. It is the journalists' church, and the crypt includes a display of journalism, as well as Roman ruins.

St Clement Danes, Trafalgar Square: This stands just outside the City boundary, and a church has been on this site since it was started by the Danes in the ninth century. It was rebuilt by Wren after the Great Fire, and again after the bombing of World War II. It is the church of the Royal Air Force and, to some extent, of the USAAF.

St Dunstan-in-the-West, Fleet Street: This church celebrates the tenth-century Archbishop of Canterbury, who was also a goldsmith.

St Giles-in-the-Field, Flitcroft Street, W1: This church was for some time the last stop for criminals on their way to execution.

St James, Piccadilly: A fine Wren church with a brass-rubbing centre. It was restored after wartime bombing.

St Martin-in-the-Fields, Trafalgar Square: One of the most famous of London's smaller churches for its location, the crypt and close connection with the theatre. The most important work of James Gibbs, it was completed in 1722 on the site of an earlier church, and it was restored about twenty-five years ago.

St Mary-at-the-Hill, Lovat Lane, EC3: This church was built by Wren between 1670 and 1676.

St Mary-le-Strand: A fine example of James Gibbs's work; built between 1714 and 1717.

St Stephen, Walbrook: Situated next to the Mansion House, St Stephen is one of Wren's finest works, the dome is a pattern for that of St Paul's.

It is as well to check the visiting times at churches – sightseeing is not usually allowed during services.

3

Museums

London is a city of magnificent museums, entrance to most of them being free.

British Museum
The British Museum is probably the largest and richest museum in the world, containing approximately 8 million objects from all parts of the globe. It was founded by Parliament to house the bequest of Hans Sloane – a collection of priceless manuscripts – and the contents of the Royal Library. Dating from 1753, the museum was opened at Montague House in 1759, but this became too small for the growing collection. The present building is in Classical style, the main façade being 370ft (113m) long, with a colonnade of forty-four columns. It was started in 1823 to designs by Sir Robert Smirke.

The British Museum

Among the exhibits are the Magna Carta, the Rosetta Stone, the Log Book of the *Victory*, the Elgin Marbles, and a first folio of Shakespeare, as well as countless other objects of archaeological, artistic and ethnographic interest. In 1757, George II presented the Royal Library to the museum and, in 1823, George IV conferred on it the right to a copy of every book printed in Britain. The Library, with some 6 million volumes, is open only to those who have a Reader's Pass.

OTHER MUSEUMS

Bethnal Green Museum: Fine collection of English domestic art, also a display of dolls' houses and American dolls.

British Army Museum, Royal Hospital Road, Chelsea: This includes many items from the American Revolution.

Geological Museum, Exhibition Road: One of the finest exhibitions of stones, including rare gems, in the world.

Hunterian Museum, Lincoln's Inn Fields: Founded by eighteenth-century surgeon, John Hunter, it contains 13,687 anatomical specimens.

Madame Tussauds

Victoria and Albert Museum

Imperial War Museum: This is situated in Lambeth Road on the site of what was once Bethlehem Hospital for the insane, better known as Bedlam. It contains weapons, flags and standards of two world wars, with an unequalled collection of paintings by official war artists.

Madame Tussauds, Marylebone Road: A waxwork museum of the famous and infamous figures of the past and present. The original Madame, a friend of the French royal family, fled to Britain during the Revolution with a collection of death masks which she had been forced to make of guillotined people. Later she added waxworks of English murderers.

Museum of London, London Wall: A modern museum incorporating the London and Guildhall Museums. It shows the history of London from earliest times until the present.

Museum of Mankind, behind the Royal Academy: An extension of the British Museum, it has one of the world's finest collections of primitive art.

National Maritime Museum, Greenwich: One of the most splendid buildings in London, it shows British naval history, centred round the Queen's House (Inigo Jones).

Natural History Museum, Cromwell Road: Started by Hans Sloane, it was originally part of the British Museum and moved to South Kensington in 1881. One of the largest of its type in the world, it contains specimens of all types of animals, birds, insects and reptiles from prehistoric to modern times. There are about 40 million specimens, and the number is growing every year.

National Postal Museum, King Edward Street near the Old Bailey: Though small, this is one of the finest of its kind in the world, including nearly every postage stamp issued by any postal authority since 1878.

Public Record Office, Chancery Lane: Houses the national archives, including the Domesday Book and the signatures of every British monarch.

Royal Air Force Museum, Hendon: Houses most of the types of aeroplane flown by the RAF, together with uniforms, medals etc.

Science Museum, Exhibition Road: This displays all types of mechanical and scientific appliances, dating back 200 years. There are many working models.

Victoria and Albert Museum, Cromwell Road: This occupies more than 10 acres (4ha) and contains perhaps the world's finest collection of fine and applied art. There are costumes from all ages, Middle East and Indian art, furniture, porcelain and jewellery, armour, clocks and carpets.

4

Art Galleries

National Gallery, Trafalgar Square
This is one of the world's greatest art galleries, housing works by artists such as Leonardo da Vinci, Raphael and Titian besides being particularly strong in the Dutch masters, including nineteen Rembrandts. There are also many paintings by American artists – Whistler for instance.

Built between 1832 and 1838, it is planned to extend the gallery by building on a vacant site on the west side. Special exhibitions are mounted from time to time.

National Portrait Gallery
This adjoins the National Gallery on the east side. It was founded in 1856 with the object of illustrating British history through art and through the portraits of the most famous men and women.

There are fine examples of such artists as Lely, Kneller, Romney and Reynolds, with a strong representation of American painters. Here, again, there are frequent special exhibitions.

Tate Gallery, Millbank
This houses the third of London's major art collections, namely the nation's greatest collection of modern art, with many works by artists such as Picasso, Chagall and Matisse. It is also very strong in sculpture. There are changing exhibitions of works by living artists, including much which one would find hard to classify as art.

OTHER GALLERIES TO VISIT

Courtauld Institute, Woburn Square: Has many important works of art, including Whistlers.

Dulwich College Picture Gallery, College Road, Dulwich: Has very good works by Rembrandt, Rubens and Gainsborough.

Hayward Art Gallery: Adjoining the Royal Festival Hall, this gallery holds frequent exhibitions by contemporary artists.

The National Gallery, Trafalgar Square

Institute of Contemporary Arts, Nash House, The Mall: Has changing exhibitions.

Queen's Gallery, Buckingham Palace Road: Shows items from royal collections of pictures, jewels and tapestry,

Royal Academy of Arts, Burlington House, Piccadilly: Dates from 1715, houses many fine paintings, and is famous for the annual summer exhibition.

Wallace Collection, Manchester Square: Contains Rembrandts, Rubens and Titians; also Limoges enamel work.

5

Parks

London is a city of parks, each having its own particular characteristics and its own focus of interest.

Green Park and St James's Park

Green Park's 49 acres (20ha) lie between Piccadilly and the adjoining St James's Park's 93 acres (38ha) extending from Whitehall to Buckingham Palace. They are the oldest parks in London. St James's was originally laid out by Henry VIII as a private park and did not become a public one until after the Restoration. The park is notable for the lake in the centre, with many species of wildfowl.

On the Whitehall side of the park is Horse Guards Parade, once a tiltyard, where troopers of the Life Guards mount guard daily. From here an archway leads to a wide gravelled space upon which the ceremony of Trooping the Colour takes place in June, on the official birthday of the sovereign.

Kensington Gardens

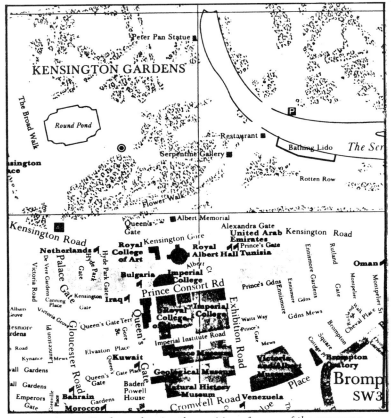

Kensington Gardens, showing the position of many of the museums

Hyde Park and Kensington Gardens

Hyde Park (341 acres, 138ha), one of the most famous parks in the world, is bounded by Park Lane, Bayswater Road and Kensington Gardens (275 acres, 111ha). At one corner is the Marble Arch, originally erected by George IV at the entrance to Buckingham Palace and placed in the present site in 1851.

Hyde Park takes its name from the manor of Hyde which was owned, until the Dissolution of the Monasteries, by Westminster Abbey. It was then taken over by Henry VIII and converted into a Royal Park then, in the reign of Charles I, made into a public one. It contains an artificial lake, the Serpentine, which is used for boating and bathing; Speaker's Corner at Marble Arch, where the world is put to rights daily; and Rotten Row for horse riding.

Kensington Gardens, notable for its beautifully laid out flower beds, also contains the Round Pond where serious model yachtsmen earnestly sail their craft, particularly on Sundays; the Albert Memorial, erected by Queen Victoria in memory of her husband; and the statue of Peter Pan. Sadly, the trees which used to line the Broad Walk, running from Bayswater to Kensington, have succumbed to Dutch elm disease; but young trees have been planted.

Regent's Park and Primrose Hill

Together these comprise 464 acres (188ha) north of Marylebone Road. Regent's Park was originally a royal hunting lodge at the time of the Commonwealth. It reverted to the Crown in 1811 and was then redesigned by John Nash for the Prince Regent, after whom it is named. It was opened to the public in 1838.

As well as the zoo, Regent's Park also contains Queen Mary's beautiful Rose Garden, an artificial lake used for sailing or rowing, and the Open Air Theatre at which one can enjoy Shakespeare's *Midsummer Night's Dream*, weather permitting! Winfield House, on the north-west corner of the park, is the official residence of the United States Ambassador.

Albert Memorial

Feeding the birds in Regent's Park

OTHER PARKS

Many other parks, either in or close to London, are worth a visit:

Alexandra Park and Palace (200 acres, 81ha): Has roller skating and a ski slope.

Battersea Park (200 acres, 81ha): Has the Festival Gardens, concert pavilion, zoo, a lake and a collection of modern sculptures.

Blackheath (271 acres, 110ha): Contains Morden College, designed by Wren. Concerts and poetry readings are held at Rangers House.

Bushey Park (1,099 acres, 445ha): Adjoins Hampton Court and contains many fine trees and avenues of horse chestnuts. Should be seen when the trees are in full bloom in early May.

Crystal Palace (199 acres, 80ha): Has a Concert Bowl and the National Sports Centre. The original building, built in 1851 for the Great Exhibition in Hyde Park, was removed to Sydenham in 1884, but was burned down in 1936. The Great Central Hall was 1,600ft (488m) in length.

Greenwich Park (196 acres, 79ha): Is best approached by launch down river from Westminster Bridge. Here is situated Greenwich Hospital, since 1873 the Royal Naval College, built by Charles II from designs by Inigo Jones, and extended by Queen Anne and William III from designs by Wren, on the site of an ancient royal palace enlarged by Humphrey, Duke of Gloucester, in the 1400s.

Henry VIII was born here and so were his daughters, Mary and Elizabeth, and Edward VI died here. Facing the college is the National Maritime Museum, behind which is the park, rising to the former Royal Observatory.

The maritime theme is continued with *Cutty Sark* (page 87), the last of the famous tea clippers, which has been fully restored with a museum of sail on board. Alongside is the yacht *Gipsy Moth IV*, in which Sir Francis Chichester sailed single handed around the world.

Hampstead Heath (825 acres, 333ha): Is an open, hilly, woody and somewhat wild area to the north of London. Many fine views of the city can be seen from the Heath, which includes the highest point in the capital. Here also is Kenwood House, remodelled by Robert Adams in the Classical style, in a park of oaks and beeches. The Iveagh bequest, in the house, includes

Hyde Park Corner (Woodmansterne Limited Watford)

a splendid art collection with Romney, Rembrandt, Turner and Gainsborough as well as many others represented, and also a magnificent Adam library. Open-air symphony concerts are held in the grounds each summer, as well as recitals in the orangery. Nearby is Hampstead village with many literary associations.

Holland Park (55 acres, 22ha): Is in Kensington and contains Holland House – the remaining wing of a seventeenth-century mansion – and an attractive orangery. Open-air concerts and plays take place here and, nearby, is the Commonwealth Institute.

6

Other Places of Historical Interest

Tower of London

Of all the other sights of London, the Tower of London is perhaps the most constantly visited. It is a grim reminder of the bloodstained and violent periods of English history. One of the most imposing fortresses in the land, it has been a keep, a fortress and a prison, and was started by William I as a stronghold to control the City and its approaches. Of the original building, the White Tower remains. It was a residence of every monarch until 1625, except for Elizabeth I who had been imprisoned there for a time by Mary I. The castle has been altered and added to, by subsequent monarchs and, until the time of Oliver Cromwell, was a royal palace.

The White Tower is surrounded by an inner ward, enclosed by a great wall flanked by thirteen towers. This in turn is further protected by an outer ward with six towers, which was formerly encircled by a moat.

The history of the Tower of London is closely bound up with the history of the country, and it was for a long time a place of execution of political prisoners, and those who offended the monarch of the time. Among the famous heads which have rolled are two queens of Henry VIII – Anne Boleyn and Katherine Howard, Sir Thomas More, Lady Jane Grey and Sir Walter Ralegh. Some of those executed were buried in the chapel of St Peter ad Vincula, the chapel of the Tower. Kings of England, France and Scotland have been imprisoned here, along with countless others, and here the two tragic young sons of Edward IV – Edward V and Richard, Duke of York – are generally supposed to have been murdered. Many of those who came to be imprisoned or executed arrived by river through Traitor's Gate.

The Tower is now an armoury and the repository of the Crown Jewels. Most of the regalia was melted down during the Commonwealth, and nearly all the present collection dates from the Restoration. Formerly the Tower housed the Observatory and the Royal Mint. It is commanded by a high-ranking army officer, who bears the title of the 'Constable of the Royal Palace and the Fortress of London'. His duties are not onerous,

The Bank of England

the administration being carried out mostly by the Resident Governor supported by forty Yeoman Warders, sometimes called 'Beefeaters', who still wear a uniform of Tudor origin.

Baker Street: Has no particular importance, except in fiction. No 221B was where the world's most famous 'private eye', Sherlock Holmes, had his lodgings. Of the present numbers, either 61 or 109–11 seems the most likely site of 221B.

Bank of England: Otherwise known as 'The Old Lady of Threadneedle Street', this is still probably the most important bank in the world, and is the repository of Britain's gold reserves. It was founded in 1694, and moved to the present site in 1736 – a building designed by Sir John Soane. Some parts may be visited by special arrangement.

Barbican: A short distance from London's meat market, Smithfield, this is an ambitious undertaking, a redevelopment of an area devastated by bombs in World War II.

The Barbican

Buckingham Palace

It comprises commercial and residential property, and also a large cultural centre which is a home of the Royal Shakespeare Company and the London Symphony Orchestra. There are also cafés, cinemas and an art gallery. Included in the area is the 600-year-old church of St Giles, Cripplegate.

Belgrave Square: One of the most handsome in London, housing a number of embassies. The term 'Belgravia', with its connection with high society, refers to the square and the immediate neighbourhood.

Berkeley Square: Here, where, as the song says, 'the nightingale sang', is the heart of Mayfair, one of London's most fashionable districts. The square consists of commercial rather than residential property nowadays. No 50 is supposed to be the most haunted house in London.

Bloomsbury Square: Noted for its literary connections, though most of the coterie which made up the 'Bloomsbury' set lived in other squares in the area.

Bond Street: One of the most fashionable, as well as the most expensive, shopping streets in the capital. Adjacent to it is **Burlington Arcade,** with equally expensive shops. This was built in 1819 for the purpose of 'giving employment to industrious females'.

Buckingham Palace: The residence of the monarch in London, this is situated at the west end of St James's Park and was originally built as a private home of John Sheffield, created Duke of Buckingham by Queen Anne in 1703. George III bought it for his wife, Queen Charlotte, in 1762, and it became the royal palace during the reign of Queen Victoria.

One of the most popular sights of London, the Changing of the Guard at the palace takes place daily between May and October, and on alternate days during the rest of the year. The ceremony takes place on the park side, which is actually the rear of the building. The front faces a 40 acre (16ha) garden, in which the queen holds a series of garden parties during the summer.

The palace is not open to the public who can, however, on occasions, visit the Royal Mews to see the royal coaches and transport.

Bush House: In the Strand, this is of particular interest to American visitors, having been designed by an American architect and erected by Irving Bush of New York. The building, dedicated to the 'Friendship of English Speaking Peoples', houses the British Broadcasting Corporation's World Service.

Chelsea Royal Hospital: Was designed by Sir Christopher Wren in 1682 as an institution for veteran and invalided soldiers. Known as Chelsea Pensioners, they can be identified by their red coats. The grounds, chapel and great hall can be visited for a few hours daily. Nearby is **Cheyne Walk,** where Whistler lived and painted the portrait of his mother.

College of Arms, or Heralds' College: In Queen Victoria Street in the City, this is the official repository of English coats of arms and pedigrees. The Officers of Arms were first incorporated by Richard III, and housed on the present site during the reign of Mary I. The building now in use was built after the Great Fire of 1666.

Covent Garden: Lies north of the Strand and used to be the convent garden of Westminster Abbey. After the Reformation, the property passed to the Duke of Somerset, and later to the Duke of Bedford, who commissioned Inigo Jones to develop it. It was modelled on the piazza at Leghorn, Italy. In 1671, by Royal Charter, it became a small market, which was gradually extended to become the largest fruit, flower and vegetable market in the country. This was moved south of the Thames in 1974, and the area was redeveloped, with shops, pubs, restaurants and also the London Transport Museum. Nearby is the church of St Paul, built by Inigo Jones but rebuilt in 1798.

Downing Street: Off Whitehall, this includes No 10, the official town residence of the Prime Minister and No 11, of the Chancellor of the Exchequer. The street is named after Sir George Downing, soldier and diplomat, who was a Member of Parliament from 1660 until 1684. Downing, who went to America at the age of fifteen, was the second man to graduate from Harvard. He served both Cromwell and Charles II.

Fleet Street: A continuation of the Strand, it is named after the Fleet river, which used to join the Thames at Blackfriars. The street was the home of most of Britain's national newspapers; now most have moved.

Grosvenor Square, Roosevelt Statue

Goldsmith's Hall: Foster Lane in the City is the site of this, perhaps the most interesting, of the halls of the City Guilds. It contains a superb collection of worked gold, open to the public, but only four times a year.

Grosvenor Square: Might also be called a piece of the United States in London. Dominated by the Embassy, with its huge gilded American Eagle, the square has had American connections ever since John Adams, the first United States Minister to Britain, and later President, took up residence there.

In the middle of the square, there is a fine statue of Franklin D. Roosevelt designed by Sir William Reid Dick. The statue was paid for by public subscription, open only to Britons, with no one to donate more than 5s (less than $1). The £200,000 needed was raised in twenty-four hours.

Guildhall: Off Gresham Street, this has been the scene of civic government for the City for more than 500 years. Built 1411–25, damaged in the Great Fire, and by incendiary bombs in 1940, the main hall and the crypt have been restored.

Events in the Guildhall include the annual election of the Lord Mayor and Sheriffs, receptions in the honour of Sovereigns and Heads of State, and meetings of the Court of Common Council. It is open to the public on weekdays. So, too, are the adjoining library, art gallery and museum of the Clockmakers' Company, which mainly escaped war damage.

Hampton Court: This magnificent palace, which can be reached either by river, bus or underground, was built by Cardinal Wolsey in 1515. After his fall from grace it was taken over by Henry VIII as a royal palace. There is a fine picture gallery and imposing state rooms, enormous tapestries, and a good collection of weapons.

The formal gardens, beautifully laid out, include the famous maze, a tiltyard and an orangery. There is also a tennis court, built by Henry. The palace is surrounded by a large well-maintained park of some 600 acres (240ha).

Houses of Parliament and Westminster Hall: These are situated in Parliament Square. By far the oldest of these buildings is the Hall which was built by William II and modernised 200 years later by Richard II, who was responsible for the magnificent hammer-beam roof. The Hall served for centuries as a meeting place of the Courts of Law, and has been the scene of many great trials. Among those condemned to

Hampton Court

death here were Charles I, Sir Thomas More and Guy Fawkes. Here, also, Oliver Cromwell was installed as Protector. Unfortunately, for security reasons, the Hall is no longer open to the public.

The Houses of Parliament (the Palace of Westminster) stand on the site of a royal palace, which was built for Edward the Confessor, and remained the royal palace until Henry VIII moved into Whitehall Palace. Westminster Palace was destroyed by fire in 1834, and rebuilding commenced under the architect, Sir Charles Barry, in 1840. Just over 100 years later, the Commons' Chamber was destroyed by enemy action, and the new Chamber was not opened until 1950.

During the intervening period, the Commons met in the Gothic Hall in the House of Lords, designed by Augustus Pugin, who co-operated with Barry during the previous rebuilding. This Hall contains the throne of the monarch and also the Woolsack, a plain cushioned sofa which is used by the Lord Chancellor as presiding officer of the House of Lords.

At each end of the palace is a high tower – the 320ft (96m) clock tower with the most famous clock in the world, Big Ben, and the 330ft (100m) Victoria Tower, above the royal entrance, used by the sovereign at the State Opening of Parliament once a year.

The Houses of Parliament are no longer open to visitors, except by special arrangement, but the public may attend debates in the Commons in the Strangers' Gallery.

Inns of Court: There are four of these – Inner and Middle Temple, Gray's and Lincoln's. They are the centres of the legal profession, originating during the fifteenth century. By long custom the Inns enjoy the sole privilege of admitting people to practise at the Bar.

The gardens of these Inns are mostly open to the public, as are the chapels and churches therein. It was in Middle Temple Gardens, not open to the public, that Shakespeare set the scene which led to the War of the Roses. Inner and Middle Temples were originally occupied by the Knights Templars – an order of Crusaders.

Kensington Palace: Sited in Kensington Gardens, this was a royal residence between 1689 and 1760. Queen Victoria was born here, and lived here until her accession to the throne. There is a fine garden which, like some of the state apartments, is open to the public.

Kew Royal Botanical Gardens: Its 300 acres (121ha) were originally laid out in 1759 as a private garden for Kew House, occupied by the mother of George III.

There are fine greenhouses, in which plants from all over the world are grown and studied. This work has led to development of colonial economies; an example is the Malaysian rubber industry, which started with a plant from Kew imported from Brazil. The gardens are open to the public.

Lambeth Palace: This, for some 700 years, has been the London residence of the Archbishop of Canterbury. On the south bank of the Thames, the oldest part is thirteenth century. For leave to visit the historical parts, applications have to be made to the archbishop's chaplain.

Law Courts: In the Strand, these took sixteen years to build, using 80,000 tons of stone, and were opened in 1882. The main feature is the enormous Central Hall, which is 238ft (72m) long, 38ft (12m) wide and 80ft (24m) high. The Courts are for civil proceedings, not criminal cases. The public are admitted to the galleries.

London Bridge: Perhaps the most famous of the bridges over the Thames, it is the oldest, connecting the City with Southwark. It was in fact the only bridge over the river until Westminster Bridge was built in 1750. No one knows for sure the date of the original structure, but there was a wooden bridge

Law Courts

in Saxon times and quite possibly a crossing of some type in the Roman period.

The first stone bridge was started in 1176 by Henry II, but not completed until much later. In those days there were houses and shops on both sides of the bridge and a chapel in the middle. This was pulled down and a new bridge started in 1779. This was again rebuilt in 1831. When this was demolished to make way for the present structure in 1973, the facing stones were taken to Arizona, which now claims to have London Bridge.

Lord's Cricket Ground

(below left) Mansion House; *(*right*)* Old Bailey

Lord's Cricket Ground: This is the headquarters in St John's Wood of that game which has always been a source of puzzlement to Americans and others. The ground is the property of the Marylebone Cricket Club, better known as the MCC, and named after Thomas Lord, a groundsman, who selected the original ground, now Dorset Square. The present ground was opened in 1814.

There is a cricket museum on the ground, containing a fine collection of pictures and other objects connected with the game. There is also a real tennis court, one of the few in the country for this complicated and long-established game which bears little resemblance to that played at Wimbledon.

Mansion House: Is the official residence of the Lord Mayor of London and was built facing the Bank of England between 1739 and 1753. Its sumptuous interior may be visited on occasions.

Monument, The: This hollow column, built to commemorate the Great Fire of London, was designed by Wren. Its 202ft (65m) height is supposed to represent the distance from the baker's shop in Pudding Lane, where the fire started. A spiral staircase of 311 steps leads to a public gallery, from which there is a fine panoramic view of London.

Old Bailey: The Central Criminal Court, built on the site of Newgate Prison and near St Paul's, is surmounted by a dome, crowned by a 12ft (3.6m) high figure of Justice, complete with scales. The public can attend trials here.

Old Vic: This theatre in Waterloo Road, once the home of the National Theatre Company, is now owned by the American entrepreneur 'Honest Ed' Mervish.

Pall Mall: This, one of the finest nineteenth-century thoroughfares in London, running between Piccadilly and St James's Park, is the centre of 'Clubland'. It was called after the croquet-like game of 'pell-mell'.

Parliament Square: Is a good vantage point from which to view the Houses of Parliament, Westminster Abbey and Big Ben. It also has statues of Winston Churchill, Abraham Lincoln, Viscount Palmerston and General Jan Smuts.

Piccadilly Circus: A somewhat tatty roundabout, in which is the statue of Eros. The name probably derives from 'pickadill'

– a type of support for an Elizabethan ruff. Piccadilly, a handsome thoroughfare to Hyde Park Corner, and Regent Street, an imposing street of many well-known stores which goes north to Oxford Circus, both run out of Piccadilly Circus.

North of Oxford Circus, Regent Street continues to Portland Place, an imposing road laid out by the Adam brothers at the start of which are the premises (not by the Adam brothers) of the BBC. At its other end it reaches Regent's Park via Park Crescent. Portland Place houses a number of embassies and chancelleries.

Portobello Road: Is the site of one of the most interesting street markets. Like all such, most of the items on sale could be classified as junk, but some worthwhile objects may be spotted.

Post Office Tower: Between Portland Place and Tottenham Court Road, 580ft (177m) with a 40ft (12m) mast on top. Visitors used to be able to go up to the top, but for security reasons are no longer allowed.

Royal Albert Hall: This, opposite the Albert Memorial, is another example of Victorian architecture. It is best known for its concerts, including the famous Promenade Concerts during the summer.

Royal Festival Hall: Another venue for concerts and other musical performances, the Royal Festival Hall, with the adjoining **Queen Elizabeth Hall,** dates from the Festival of Britain of 1953. The best approach is by the Hungerford footbridge across the Thames.

St James's Palace: This palace, lying between St James's Park and the end of Pall Mall, was built by Henry VIII. The gatehouse and part of the chapel remain. A royal residence from 1697 to 1762, representatives of foreign powers are still accredited to the Court of St James. It is the headquarters of the Honourable Corps of Gentlemen at Arms, and the Queen's bodyguard of the Yeomen of the Guard.

Savoy Chapel: This chapel, behind the world famous Savoy Hotel, is officially the Queen's Chapel of the Savoy and is the chapel of the Royal Victorian Order. It is a private chapel of the monarch, and was originally part of the palace built in 1245 named after Count Peter of Savoy and later owned by John of Gaunt. The present chapel is Victorian.

(left) Cleopatra's Needle; *(inset left)* The Post Office Tower; *(above)* Regent
Street; *(below)* Nelson's Column and Trafalgar Square (Woodmansterne
Limited Watford)

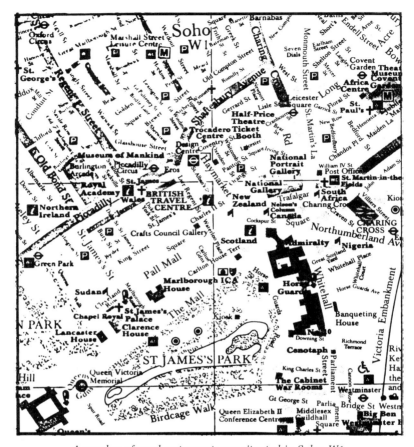

A number of good restaurants are situated in Soho, W1

Smithfield Market: Charterhouse Square is the site of this the largest meat market in the world. Nearby is St Bartholomew's Hospital.

Soho: Lying behind Piccadilly Circus, this is a rather sleazy area from which most of the old-established shops have been driven out by strip joints and sex shops. However, a number of very good restaurants are situated in Soho, and on the Charing Cross Road border there are many secondhand bookshops, including Foyle's, said to be the largest bookshop in the world.

Somerset House: The original was built in the Strand, in 1547, by the Duke of Somerset, Protector of King Edward VI.

However, he did not live long enough to complete it, being interrupted by his execution. Queen Elizabeth I lived there during the reign of her sister, Mary. Inigo Jones and Oliver Cromwell died there.

The present building, dating from 1776, was the registry of births, marriages and deaths, but this has now been dispersed and the future of the building is uncertain.

Stock Exchange: Near the Bank of England, the Stock Exchange is a modern building (completed in 1972) on the site of the previous exchange founded in 1773 for the purpose of buying and selling shares. The new building has a gallery for visitors.

Strand: Originally a strip of land by the Thames, it runs from Trafalgar Square to Fleet Street. It has many interesting and historic buildings: Somerset House, the Law Courts, the Savoy Hotel and Chapel.

Syon House: In Brentford, west London. Originally a monastery founded by Henry V, it was later acquired by the Protector, Somerset, who was accused of treason by John Dudley and executed. Dudley became Earl of Nothumberland, and took over Syon House. It was renovated and redecorated in 1750 by Robert Adam, and the garden redesigned by Capability Brown.

Tower Bridge: Was built between 1886 and 1894. The two spans of 1,000ft (305m) each are supposed never to have failed to open in 90 seconds for the passage of shipping. There is a high-level pedestrian walk, which has now been reopened after being closed for fifty years because of the number of people committing suicide from it.

Nearby, St Katherine's Dock has been rebuilt as a yacht basin, housing several famous vessels.

Trafalgar Square: Was designed by John Nash in 1820, but not completed until 1840. This is one of the most famous and impressive squares in the world. The square, around which are several large buildings including the National Gallery and the church of St Martin-in-the-Fields, is dominated by the 185ft (56m) **Nelson's Column** (designed by William Railton), with Landseer's famous lions. On the west side, leading to the Mall, is Admiralty Arch, a memorial to Queen Victoria.

Victoria Embankment: Stretches from Waterloo Bridge to Blackfriars Bridge along the Thames for about a mile (1.6km).

It offers fine views of the Festival Hall and County Hall across the Thames, and contains the pleasant little Victoria Embankment Gardens in which military bands play during the summer.

On the river side is **Cleopatra's Needle,** which is not a needle, nor has it anything to do with the famous, or infamous, queen of Egypt. It is a 68½ft (21m) high granite monolith, one of several originally set up at Heliopolis in Egypt in about 1,500BC and given to Britain as a coronation gift for George IV. Because of international disputes, it did not arrive until nearly forty-eight years after his death.

There is a similar monolith in Central Park, New York.

Whitehall: This runs from Parliament Square to Trafalgar Square and has been a thoroughfare since the fifteenth century. It has long been associated with government ministries, though many of them have moved. It is divided by the Cenotaph, the memorial to the dead of two world wars, where the monarch attends an Armistice Day Service on a Sunday every November.

Whitehall used to be the site of a royal palace which, from 1529 until it was burned down in 1698, was the chief residence of the monarch. The banqueting hall of Inigo Jones still stands, and is open for visiting. Across the road is Horse Guards Parade, once the tiltyard of the palace, now the offices of the Commander in Chief of the Home Forces.

Windsor Castle: This is the largest inhabited castle in the world, covering 13 acres (5ha). It was started in the reign of William the Conqueror and, since his time many monarchs have had a hand in the building, among them Edward III who was born in the castle. He enlarged the royal apartments and, in 1345, founded the Order of the Garter, the premier order of knighthood. The castle is made up in three parts: the Lower Ward, which includes St George's Chapel, Upper Ward, where the state apartments are located, and the enormous Round Tower.

St George's Chapel, started by Edward IV, was completed in the reign of Henry VIII, one of the many monarchs buried there with his third wife, Jane Seymour. It was constructed in the same style as Henry VII's Chapel in Westminster Abbey, with the same master masons, the brothers Vertue, involved in the construction.

The state apartments which, like the chapel, are open to the public subject to royal requirements, are utterly magnificent. They contain remarkable collections of pottery, armour, furniture, tapestries and sculpture.

Windsor Castle

The castle stands in Home Park, 400 acres (162ha) bounded by the Thames, in which is Frogmore, a private mausoleum built by Queen Victoria. This is open to the public only on two days in early May. Victoria is buried there with her husband, Prince Albert; also Edward VIII, who abdicated, becoming the Duke of Windsor.

Nearby is Windsor Great Park, an immense area of park and woodland, containing magnificent gardens and also the Long Walk of 3 miles (4.8km) ending with a statue of George III. Queen Anne, who was very fond of racing, added another 3 mile (4.8km) ride leading to Ascot racecourse, along which the royal party drive to the Royal Ascot meeting in June.

The town of Windsor is worth a visit, with attractive Georgian and Victorian buildings and a Guildhall completed by Wren.

Zoological Gardens: These, in Regent's Park, occupy an area of about 36 acres (14ha), and contain one of the finest collections of animals, birds and reptiles in the world. They were founded in 1826 and gradually expanded, the aquarium, the first of its type, being built in 1853.

Few of the original buildings survive, but among the modern buildings is a particularly fine aviary.

7

Walks

It is very often quicker to cover short distances in London on foot, rather than by taxi or other public transport. But it is worthwhile considering taking a London Transport Bus Tour, or a 'Culture' Bus Tour, which lasts about two hours.

WALK 1

Take a bus or underground to Charing Cross (Jubilee, Bakerloo or Northern Lines) and proceed down the Strand, passing Charing Cross railway station. In the forecourt of the station is a replica of the cross which marked the place where the body of Queen Eleanor of Castille spent the night on the way to burial in Westminster Abbey. The station was designed by Brunel. On the way down the Strand, you pass the famous Savoy Hotel, Waterloo Bridge and Bush House. It is worthwhile making a detour to see Covent Garden, which is on the left-hand side.

The Strand leads into Fleet Street, passing Somerset House, and with two important churches in the middle – St Mary le Strand and St Clement Danes. Among the other notable buildings are the Law Courts, Prince Henry's Room – the oldest domestic building in London (1610), and the old Cheshire Cheese pub. Just off Fleet Street lies the Temple, consisting of two Inns of Court, Inner and Middle Temple. Enter by a gateway which supports Prince Henry's Room. Also nearby is Gough Square with Dr Johnson's House at No 17.

Fleet Street, once the home of many of Britain's newspapers, leads to Ludgate Circus and Ludgate Hill, at the top of which is St Paul's Cathedral. Although somewhat spoilt by modern buildings, there is a fine view of the cathedral from Ludgate Circus. A short distance from Ludgate Hill is the Old Bailey, or Central Criminal Courts. Beyond St Paul's, Queen Victoria Street leads to the Mansion House, the Bank of England and the nearby Stock Exchange.

The Tower of London is not far away from here and can be approached by several routes. One way leads via Cornhill, Leadenhall Street, passing Lloyds of London, and Aldgate. Another route takes one past the Monument and Eastcheap to Tower Hill.

Charing Cross

Adjoining the Tower is St Katherine's Dock, a converted corner of London's docklands. This includes a collection of ancient ships, London's trade centre, and the Dickens Inn, well converted from an ancient warehouse.

There are several buses from the Tower, as well as Tower Hill station which is on the Circle and District Lines.

WALK 2

Take a bus or the underground to Piccadilly Circus (Piccadilly and Bakerloo Lines). The circus is a prime example of the changing face of London. Although the most visited spot in the city, it is one of the most unpleasant, so do not bother to stay long. Have a look at the statue of Eros, then proceed along Coventry Street to Leicester Square, where the second Earl of Leicester was given permission to build a mansion (finished in 1631), provided that he left a green square where the peasants could do their washing.

St Katherine's Dock

Whitehall (Woodmansterne Limited Watford)

Two American artists are associated with the square; John Singleton Copley had his studio at No 12, after arriving from America in 1774; and John Trumbull lived at No 29. Sir Joshua Reynolds had his residence at what is now Fanum House, the headquarters of the Automobile Association, while William Hogarth died at No 30. Several large cinemas are located here, and also a theatre ticket booth, and there are statues of William Shakespeare and Sir Charles (Charlie) Chaplin.

Walk down Charing Cross Road towards Trafalgar Square, passing the statue of Nurse Edith Cavell, World War I heroine. The National Portrait Gallery is on your right, facing the Nelson column with the statue of Lord Horatio and, beyond, Admiralty Arch. There are several other notable statues hereabouts, including a fine equestrian one of George III in Cockspur Street, and a bronze one of James II. The church by the square is St Martin-in-the-Fields. Nowadays Trafalgar Square is a meeting place for demonstrations and political meetings. On every New Year's Eve there are celebrations – noisy but generally good humoured.

Proceed down Whitehall towards Parliament Square, passing Horseguards Parade and Downing Street on the right, and the Banqueting House on the left. Whitehall is divided by the Cenotaph, a monument to those who gave their lives in the two world wars, and also contains some interesting statues, among them General Montgomery and Sir Walter Ralegh. Whitehall enters Parliament Square on the north side, facing Westminster Abbey, with the Palace of Westminster (the Houses of Parliament) and Big Ben on the left. In the square will be found statues of Abraham Lincoln, by Augustus St Gaudens; Jan Christian Smuts, by Jacob Epstein; and Ivor Roberts-Jones's Sir Winston Churchill.

From here, depending upon time or energy, there are alternative routes:

Route A   Along Victoria Embankment for about 1½ miles (2.4km) from Westminster Bridge to Blackfriars Bridge, beside the Thames with fine views of the Royal Festival Hall over the river and, ahead, St Paul's Cathedral.

On the way you will pass Cleopatra's Needle, the Victoria Embankment Gardens with a statue of James McNeill Whistler, and one or two old ships. At Blackfriars there is an underground station on the Circle and District Lines.

Route B   Via St James's Park and Buckingham Palace. Enter the park from the west side of the square and Birdcage Walk, which leads to the palace, the London home of the queen – in residence when the flag is flying. Here you can see the ceremony of the Changing of the Guard, which takes place daily during summer, and on alternate days in winter, unless it is raining. The ceremony takes place at 11.30am, but get there early if you want a decent view.

Walk down the Mall back to Trafalgar Square through Admiralty Arch, but do look back for the vista of the palace at the end of the Mall.

From Trafalgar Square there are buses to most parts of London.

WALK 3

Take a bus or the underground's Piccadilly Line to Knightsbridge, one of London's major shopping centres. Knightsbridge was, until 1800, a small village, built round a bridge over the River Westbourne on the main road to London. The village began to grow and in 1813 Benjamin Harvey opened his linen-draper's business, now Harvey Nichol, and in 1849 a Mr Harrod took over a grocery – the start of the famous store which still bears his name. Harrods is actually in Brompton Road, together with a number of other exclusive shops. Further down the road is Brompton Oratory, one of the biggest Roman Catholic churches in the country.

Brompton Road later leads to Thurloe Place and Cromwell Road, so called because of a legend that Oliver Cromwell once had a cottage at the Earl's Court end. This is museum country, starting with the Victoria and Albert, occupying a large site on the corner of Cromwell Road and Exhibition Road, in which also can be found the Science Museum. Further along Cromwell Road is the Natural History Museum, between Exhibition Road and Queen's Gate. Turning right, Queen's Gate leads to Kensington Road and Hyde Park, passing the Geological Museum. Right again at Kensington Road brings one to the Royal Albert Hall, one of London's most famous concert halls. Opposite, in the park, is the Albert Memorial, unveiled in 1876 by Queen Victoria as a memorial to her late husband, who is seated holding a copy of the *Catalogue* for the Great Exhibition of 1851. Designed by Sir Gilbert Scott, the spire is 175ft (53m) high, and on the base is a frieze of figures of great contemporaries.

In summer it is worthwhile making a diversion to see the flowers in the beautiful Kensington Gardens which lie to the

Dickens House

west of the memorial. Otherwise continue eastwards past Rotten Row, famous for horse riding, until you reach Hyde Park Corner. Here can be found Apsley House, presented in 1815 to the Duke of Wellington, who died here in 1852. Apsley House used to be referred to as 'No 1 London', as it was the first house reached by a traveller after passing the old turnpike gate on London's western boundary.

WALK 4

This features the London Silver Jubilee Walkway, which was created to celebrate the 25th Anniversary of the accession to the throne of Queen Elizabeth in 1952. The complete route is about 10 miles (16km), so it is better done in sections. A detailed map of the Walkway can be obtained from London Passenger Transport Board offices.

Besides the individual walks already described, there are several organised walks, with guides to take you around, and for which a payment is required. Among them are specialist walks such as Dickens's London, Literary London etc. There is usually a selection advertised daily in *The Times*. Also worth consideration, during the summer, are Canal Walks. A leaflet can be obtained from the London Tourist Board, 26 Grosvenor Gardens, London SW1.

Finally, a word of warning. London, like many cities, is changing rapidly and many landmarks are disappearing.

8

Do's and Don'ts and Hints for Visitors

1 Try to change your money at regular banks, not at hotels or small money-changing shops. You will get a better rate at banks.

2 Be extremely careful about carrying a large amount of money. It is better to leave traveller's cheques and passports in your hotel safe. Avoid carrying a wallet in your back pocket or a purse in your handbag.

3 Have the hotel porter confirm your onward or return flight as soon as possible after arrival.

4 On day of departure settle your hotel bill before 12 noon. This is the checkout time of all London hotels.

5 Check restaurant bills to see if service charge is included. If so, no tip is needed.

6 If any documents are lost or stolen, report to nearest police station.

7 If medical attention is required, your hotel will be able to put you in touch with a doctor. If you need any special medicines, bring them with you. They are probably available in Britain, but likely to be under another name. Dental treatment is expensive but good.

8 Religious services: details of the various denominational services can be obtained from your hotel.

9 Take no electrical equipment with you, unless it has adjustable voltage.

10 Money: British currency is based on the pound sterling, which is subject to considerable fluctuation vis-à-vis the dollar. Any bank will tell you the exchange rate. The pound is divided into 100 pence. There are notes of £50, £20, £10, £5. There is a £1 coin; other coins are 50 pence, 20 pence, 10 pence and 5 pence alloy coins, as well as copper coins for 1 pence and 2 pence. There is not much to be bought with the copper pieces. It is as well to bring at least £30 in currency to take care of immediate expenses, such as tips, fares etc.

11 Restaurants and cafés: it is possible to enjoy cuisine from every part of the world in London. Many restaurants now serve fixed price meals, exclusive of wine, which can be expensive.

Never buy unless a price list is shown. For good value try pubs or wine bars, but these usually serve only lunches. A number of publications such as the *Good Food Guide* are worth consulting, but the best guide is a personal recommendation. Avoid vans selling ice creams and hot dogs in the West End and other tourist spots.

12 Pubs: there are many of these, catering for all tastes and, here again, personal recommendation is best. The legal licensing hours during the week are from 11am to 11pm, but not all pubs are in fact open all this time. On Sundays the hours are from noon until 3.00pm and 7pm until 10.30pm. English beer is mostly too warm for American taste, but most pubs serve draught lager, which closely resembles American beer.

13 Toilet facilities or public conveniences can be quite hard to find and are not always very clean. They can be found at railway stations, hotels, departmental stores and some underground stations. Many of them require small coins.

14 Travelling in London can be by bus, underground, taxi or – and its worth making the effort – by foot. Buses are fairly cheap, underground slightly less cheap, taxis fairly expensive, and foot is free. If possible do not travel in the rush hour, ie 8.30–9.30am and 5.00–6.00pm.

One can obtain maps of the underground and bus routes on request from London Transport. Places outside London can be reached either by British Rail from one of the London termini, or by coaches.

15 Visitors to London are frequently approached by people purporting to be guides. The latter will often take money as a deposit for a future tour and that is the last that will be seen of them and the money.

Make sure that you deal only with official guides, passed by the Tourist Board. These guides have to pass a stringent test after which they receive a blue badge, with their name on it. They know their job, so refuse to use any other.

ENTERTAINMENT

Opera and Ballet
The Royal Opera and Royal Ballet at the Royal Opera House, Covent Garden. Daily from Monday to Saturday.
The English National Opera Company at the Coliseum Theatre, St Martin's Lane. Daily Monday to Saturday.
New Sadler's Wells Opera, Rosebery Avenue, EC1. Monday to Saturday.

The National Theatre

Theatres
There are about forty theatres open in London, most of them in the area bounded by the Strand, Kingsway and Piccadilly Circus. Apart from these, the National Theatre is across the Thames, near Waterloo, and the Royal Shakespeare Company is at the Barbican in the City, as well as at the Aldwych.

Seats can be obtained from numerous ticket agencies and the theatre bureau in Leicester Square.

Concerts
Royal Festival Hall, York Road.
Royal Albert Hall, Kensington Gore.
Wigmore Hall, Wigmore Street.
Conway Hall, Red Lion Square.

In summer, open air concerts are held at Holland Park, Kensington; Crystal Palace, Sydenham; and at Kenwood House, Hampstead Heath.

Cinemas
There are about thirty cinemas either in or near the West End.

They are open seven days a week although, on Sundays, they do not open until afternoon. Foreign films are usually sub-titled rather than dubbed.

Several publications give information about what is showing and performed in London. The London Tourist Board and the British Tourist Authority will give you any information, and there are periodicals such as *Time Out* and *What's on in London* as well as the entertainments guide in the daily newspapers.

SHOPS AND MARKETS

There are several well-defined shopping areas in London. Perhaps the best known shopping street is Bond Street with its fashion shops for men and women, its art shops and also the famous Aspreys (for those with large bank accounts). Parallel to Bond Street is the Burlington Arcade, full of exclusive men's and women's shops, fashion boutiques and objets d'art. Bond Street runs from Piccadilly (in which can be found the supreme food store Fortnum and Mason, and Simpsons for clothing) and Oxford Street, where the main stores are Selfridges, Dickins and Jones and John Lewis. Also in Oxford Street are branches of Marks and Spencer, Woolworth and British Home Stores, as well as many multiple shoe stores. Near Oxford Circus is Liberty and in Regent Street, between Oxford Circus and Piccadilly, there is Dickins and Jones, Hamley (for toys), Lawley (for china) and Austin Reed (for clothing) among many others.

A little further afield are Knightsbridge, with Harrods and Harvey Nichol; Sloane Square with Peter Jones; and Kensington High Street with John Barker.

There are a number of street markets, either specialised or general. Some of the best known are: **Petticoat Lane,** open on Sunday mornings in Middlesex Street, near Aldgate, where you may find anything; **Portobello Road,** Ladbroke Grove, where one can buy rubbish or bargains, open Saturdays; **Bermondsey Market,** Tower Bridge Road, open Wednesdays; **Covent Garden,** open weekdays; and **Camden Passage,** open Thursdays and Saturdays. These can be described as 'flea markets', though some good stuff can be found by those who know their onions.

For the upper end of the antique and art market, apart from the numerous antique shops and art galleries, several auction houses hold frequent sales, such as Sothebys in New Bond Street; Christies, St James's Place, and Philips Son and Neale.

9

Kings and Queens

Name	Accession	Death	Married	Buried
Saxons and Danes				
Egbert	827	839		
Ethelwulf	839	858		Winchester Cathedral
Ethelbald	858	860		Sherborne Abbey
Ethelbert	860	866		Reculver Abbey ruins
Ethelred (Saint)	866	871		Wimborne Abbey
Alfred the Great	871	899	Ealswyth of Gaini	1 Winchester Cathedral 2 Hyde Abbey. Bones dispersed at Reformation
Edward the Elder	899	925	1 Egwyn 2 Elfled 3 Eadgifu	Winchester Cathedral
Athelstan	925	940		Malmesbury Abbey
Edmund	940	946	1 Elgifu 2 Ethelfled	Glastonbury Abbey
Edred	946	955		Winchester Cathedral
Edwy	955	959		Winchester Cathedral
Edgar	959	975	1 Ethelfled 2 Elfthryth	Glastonbury Abbey
Edward the Martyr	975	978		1 Wareham 2 Shaftesbury Abbey
Ethelred the Unready	978	1016	1 Elfgifu 2 Emma of Normandy	Old St Paul's (destroyed in Great Fire of London)
Edmund Ironside	1016	1016		Glastonbury Abbey
Canute the Dane	1017	1035	1 Elfgifu of Deiara 2 Emma, widow of Ethelred	Winchester Cathedral
Harold	1035	1040		In church on site of St Clement Danes
Hardicanute	1040	1042		Winchester Cathedral
Edward the Confessor	1042	1066	Edith, daughter of Earl Godwin	Westminster Abbey
Harold Godwinson	1066	1066		Waltham Abbey?
Normans				
William I	1066	1087	Matilda of Flanders	Caen (France); also Matilda
William II	1087	1100	Unmarried	Winchester Cathedral
Henry I	1100	1135	1 Matilda of Scotland	Reading Abbey Brain, Rouen (France).

Name	Accession	Death	Married	Buried
			2 Adelica of Louvaine	Matilda: Westminster Abbey Adelica: Affingham Convent, Flanders
Stephen	1135	1154	Matilda of Boulogne	Faversham Abbey, (destroyed at Dissolution), also Matilda

House of Plantagenet

Name	Accession	Death	Married	Buried
Henry II	1154	1189	Eleanor of Guienne, divorced wife of Louis VII of France	Fontevraud Abbey; also Eleanor
Richard I	1189	1199	Berengaria of Navarre	Fontevraud Abbey, heart at Rouen. Berengaria: Le Mans Abbey, France (converted into a barn)
John	1199	1216	1 Avisa of Gloucester 2 Isabella of Angoulême	Worcester Cathedral Isabella: Fontevraud Abbey
Henry III	1216	1272	Eleanor of Provence	Westminster Abbey. Eleanor: Amesbury Convent, Wilts (destroyed)
Edward I	1272	1307	1 Eleanor of Castille 2 Margaret of France	Westminster Abbey; also Eleanor
Edward II	1307	1327	Isabella of France	Gloucester Cathedral. Isabella: Christ Church, Newgate St (destroyed)
Edward III	1327	1377	Philippa of Hainault	Westminster Abbey, also Philippa
Richard II	1377	1399	1 Anne, daughter of Emperor Charles IV 2 Isabel of France	Westminster Abbey, also Anne. Isabella: Bois, France

House of Lancaster

Name	Accession	Death	Married	Buried
Henry IV	1399	1413	1 Mary de Bohun 2 Joan of Navarre	Canterbury Cathedral. Mary: Holy Trinity Hospital Chapel, Leicester Joan: Canterbury Cathedral

Name	Accession	Death	Married	Buried
Henry V	1413	1422	Catherine of Valois	Westminster Abbey, also Catherine
Henry VI	1422	1461	Margaret of Anjou	St George's Chapel, Windsor
	1470	1471	Margaret	Angers Cathedral, France

House of York

Edward IV	1461	1470	Elizabeth Woodville	St George's Chapel, Windsor, also Elizabeth
	1471	1483		
Edward V	1483	1483	Unmarried	Westminster Abbey
Richard III	1483	1485	Anne, daughter of Earl of Warwick	Grey Friars, Leicester (destroyed at Dissolution). Anne: Westminster Abbey

House of Tudor

Henry VII	1485	1509	Elizabeth of York	Westminster Abbey, also Elizabeth
Henry VIII	1509	1547		St George's Chapel, Windsor. Wives:
			1 Catherine of Aragon	Peterborough Cathedral (tomb destroyed)
			2 Anne Boleyn	St Peter ad Vincula, Tower of London
			3 Jane Seymour	St George's Chapel, Windsor
			4 Anne of Cleves	Westminster Abbey
			5 Catherine Howard	St Peter ad Vincula
			6 Katherine Parr	Castle Sudeley, Glos (tomb destroyed, new tomb 1858)
Edward VI	1547	1553	Unmarried	Westminster Abbey
Jane	1553	Reigned 9 days		St Peter ad Vincula, Tower of London
Mary I	1553	1558	Philip II of Spain	Westminster Abbey. Philip: The Escorial, Madrid
Elizabeth I	1558	1603	Unmarried	Westminster Abbey

House of Stuart

James I (James VI of Scotland)	1603	1625	Anne of Denmark	Westminster Abbey, also Anne
Charles I	1625	1649	Henrietta Maria of France	St George's Chapel, Windsor. Henrietta: St Denis, Paris; heart in convent at Chaillot

Name	Accession	Death	Married	Buried
Commonwealth	1649	1660		
Charles II	1660	1685	Catherine of Braganza	Westminster Abbey. Catherine: Belem, Portugal
James II	1685	1688	1 Anne Hyde 2 Mary of Modena	Paris. Anne: Westminster Abbey Mary: Chaillot Abbey, France
William III and	1689	1702	Mary II	Westminster Abbey
Mary II	1689	1694		Westminster Abbey
Anne	1702	1714	George of Denmark	Westminster Abbey, also George
House of Hanover				
George I	1714	1727	Sophia Dorothea of Celle	Hanover. Sophia: Celle, Germany
George II	1727	1760	Caroline of Branden-burg-Anspach	Westminster Abbey, also Caroline
George III	1760	1820	Charlotte of Mecklen-burg-Strelitz	St George's Chapel, Windsor, also Charlotte
George IV	1820	1830	1 Mrs Fitzherbert (morganatic) 2 Caroline of Brunswick-Wolfen-buttel	St George's Chapel, Windsor. Caroline: Brunswick, Germany
William IV	1830	1837	Adelaide of Saxe-Coburg and Meiningen	St George's Chapel, Windsor, also Adelaide
Victoria	1837	1901	Albert of Saxe-Coburg-Gotha	Frogmore, Windsor, also Albert
House of Saxe-Coburg				
Edward VII	1901	1910	Alexandra of Denmark	St George's Chapel, Windsor, also Alexandra
House of Windsor				
George V	1910	1936	Mary of Teck	St George's Chapel, Windsor, also Mary
Edward VIII	1936	1936	Mrs Wallis Simpson	Frogmore, Windsor
George VI	1936	1952	Elizabeth Bowes-Lyon	St George's Chapel, Windsor
Elizabeth II	1952		Philip Mountbatten	

10
Burial Places of Famous People

IN LONDON

Adam, Robert	Architect	Westminster Abbey
Addison, Joseph	Essayist	Westminster Abbey
Ainsworth, Harrison	Author	Kensal Green Cemetery
Alma-Tadema, Sir Lawrence	Artist	St Paul's Cathedral
André, Major John	Hanged as a spy in American Revolutionary War	Westminster Abbey
Arne, Dr Thomas	Composer, 'Rule Britannia'	St Paul's, Covent Garden (B 6, 15, 77)
Attlee, Clement	Prime Minister	Westminster Abbey
Banks, Sir Thomas	Sculptor	St Mary's, Paddington Green, Edgware Road (B 6, 8, 16)
Barbirolli, Sir John	Conductor	St Mary's, Kensal Green (B 18)
Beatty, David 1st Earl	Admiral, World War I	St Paul's Cathedral
Beerbohm, Max	Caricaturist and writer	St Paul's Cathedral
Beeton, Mrs	Cookery books	Norwood Cemetery, High St (B 68, 172, 196)
Bessemer, Henry	Engineer, steel	Norwood Cemetery (as above)
Blake, William	Poet and artist	Bunhill Fields
Bligh, Captain William	Mutiny on the *Bounty*	St Mary's Lambeth (B 3,159)
Blondin, Charles	Crossed Niagara Falls on a tight-rope	Kensal Green Cemetery
Blood, Colonel Thomas	Stealer of the Crown Jewels	Christ Church, Broadway, Victoria St (B 1, 24, 29)
Boadicea	Queen of Iceni (a British Tribe), first century AD	Platform 10, King's Cross Station
Booth, William	Founder of the Salvation Army	Abney Park Cemetery, Church St, Stoke Newington (B 73)
Borrow, George	Author	Brompton Cemetery (U Earls Court: B 16, 30)
Browning, Robert	Poet	Westminster Abbey
Brunel, Sir Isaac	Engineer	Kensal Green Cemetery
Brunel, Isambard Kingdom	Engineer, bridge builder, son of Sir Isaac	Kensal Green Cemetery
Bunyan, John	Author, *Pilgrim's Progress*	Bunhill Fields
Burbage, Richard	Actor	St Leonard's, Shoreditch (B 6, 72)

Butler, Samuel	Author, *Hudibras*	St Paul's, Covent Garden (B 6, 15, 77)
Canning, George	Prime Minister	Westminster Abbey
Cassell, Thomas	Publisher	Kensal Green Cemetery
Caxton, William	First English printer	St Margaret's Church, Westminster
Chaucer, Geoffrey	Author, *Canterbury Tales*	Westminster Abbey
Chippendale, Thomas	Furniture maker	St Martin-in-the-Fields, Trafalgar Square
Cochrane, Thomas 10th Earl of Dundonald	Admiral in British Navy; commanded Chilean and Brazilian fleets	Westminster Abbey
Coleridge, Samuel Taylor	Poet	St Margaret's Church, Highgate (B 210, 214, 271)
Collins, Wilkie	Author	Kensal Green Cemetery
Constable, John	Artist	St John's, Hampstead (U Hampstead)
Copley, John	Artist	Highgate Cemetery
Crapper, Thomas	Plumber, developed modern WC system	Crystal Palace Cemetery, Nr Beckenham
Cromwell, Oliver	Parliamentary general in Civil War, later Lord Protector of England	St Peter ad Vincula, Tower of London
Cromwell, Thomas	Henry VIII's chancellor	St Peter ad Vincula, Tower of London
Dickens, Charles	Novelist	Westminster Abbey
Duval, Claude	Highwayman	St Paul's, Covent Garden (B 6, 15, 77)
Dyer, Sir Edward	Poet	Southwark Cathedral (B 501, 513)
Eliot, George (Mary Ann Croft)	Author	Highgate Cemetery (new)
Faraday, Michael	Electrical engineer	Highgate Cemetery
Fielding, Sir John	Magistrate, Bow St runners	Chelsea Old Church (B 39, 137)
Fleming, Alexander	Discoverer of penicillin	St Paul's Cathedral
Fletcher, John	Dramatist	Southwark Cathedral (B 501, 513)
Fox, Charles James	Statesman, opponent of Pitt the Younger	Westminster Abbey
Fox, George	Founder of the Quakers	Bunhill Fields
Foxe, John	*Book of Martyrs*	St Giles, Cripplegate (U Moorgate)
Friese-Green, William	Father of the movies	Highgate Cemetery (new)
Gainsborough, Thomas	Artist	Kew Green (U Kew Bridge: B 27)
Garrick, David	Actor	Westminster Abbey
Gibbons, Grinling	Wood carver	St Paul's, Covent Garden (B 6, 15, 77)
Godfrey, Cardinal	Catholic Archbishop of London	Westminster Cathedral (U Victoria)
Goldsmith, Oliver	Writer	Temple Church, Fleet St (U Temple: B 6, 1, 15)

Gordon, Lord George	Popery riots 1780	St James's Church. Site occupied by Euston Station
Gresham, Sir Thomas	Banker, founder Royal Exchange	St Helen's, Bishopsgate (U Liverpool St: B 6, 22)
Grey, Henry, Duke of Suffolk	Father of Lady Jane	St Peter ad Vincula, Tower of London
Grimaldi, Joseph	Clown	St James's, Pentonville Rd (U King's Cross: B 8, 30, 73, 214)
Gwynne, Nell	One of Charles I's many mistresses	Old St Martin-in-the-Fields (destroyed)
Hall, Radcliffe (Mabel Veronica Butler)	Author, *The Well of Loneliness*	Highgate Cemetery (old)
Handel, George Frederick	Musican/composer	Westminster Abbey
Hardy, Thomas	Novelist	Westminster Abbey Heart: Stinsford, Dorset
Hazlitt, William	Essayist	St Ann's, Wardour Street, now garden (U Piccadilly)
Hill, Sir Rowland	Originator of Penny Post	Westminster Abbey
Hilliard, Nicholas	Painter of miniatures	Old St Martin-in-the-Fields (destroyed)
Hinsley, Cardinal	Catholic Archbishop of London	Westminster Cathedral
Hogarth, William	Painter	St Nicholas, Chiswick (B 27)
Holbein, Hans	Painter	St Catherine Cree, Leadenhall St (destroyed)
Hood, Thomas	Poet	Kensal Green Cemetery
Hooker, Sir Joseph	Botanist	Kew (U Kew Gardens)
Howe, William Viscount	Led British troops at Bunker Hill	Twickenham (now park)
Hunt, James Leigh	Critic, poet	Kensal Green Cemetery
Hunt, William Holman	Artist	St Paul's Cathedral
Hunter, Sir John	Founder of modern surgery	1 St Martin-in-the-Fields 2 Westminster Abbey
Irving, Sir Henry	Actor	Westminster Abbey
Jeffreys, Lord George	'Hanging' judge	St Mary the Virgin, Love Lane, Aldermanbury (destroyed)
Jellicoe, Admiral Lord John	Fleet commander World War I	St Paul's Cathedral
John of Gaunt	Fourth son of Edward III; founder of House of Lancaster	Old St Paul's (destroyed)
Johnson, Dr Samuel	Lexicographer	Westminster Abbey
Jones, Inigo	Architect	St Benet, Paul's Wharf (destroyed)
Jonson, Ben	Dramatist	Westminster Abbey
Kipling, Rudyard	Author	Westminster Abbey
Lamb, Charles	Essayist, *Essays of Elia*	Edmonton, Enfield London Graveyard

Lamb, Mary	Essayist, sister of Charles	Same as brother
Landseer, Sir Edwin	Nelson's lions, Trafalgar Square	St Paul's Cathedral
Law, Andrew Bonar	Prime Minister	Westminster Abbey
Lawrence, Sir Thomas	Artist	St Paul's Cathedral
Lely, Sir Peter	Painter	St Paul's, Covent Garden (B 6, 15, 77)
Lister, Lord Joseph	Founder of antiseptic surgery	West Hampstead Cemetery, Fortune Green Road (U West Hampstead: B 26, 113)
Livingston, David	Explorer	Westminster Abbey Heart: Africa
Lloyd, Marie	Music hall artiste	West Hampstead Cemetery, Fortune Green Road (U West Hampstead: B 26, 113)
Lovelace, Richard	Poet	St Bride's, Fleet Street (B 6, 9, 11, 15)
Lytton, Edward George, Earl	Writer, *Last Days of Pompeii*	Westminster Abbey
Manning, Cardinal	Catholic Archbishop of London	Westminster Cathedral (U Victoria)
Marvell, Andrew	Poet	St Giles-in-the-Fields (U Tottenham Court Road: B 8, 25)
Masefield, John	Poet	Westminster Abbey
Marx, Karl	Political theorist, *Das Kapital*	Highgate Cemetery
Maxim, Sir Hiram	Inventor of machine gun	Norwood Cemetery, High St (B 68, 172, 196)
Millais, Sir John Everett	Painter	St Paul's Cathedral
Milton, John	Poet	St Giles, Cripplegate (U Moorgate)
More, Sir Thomas (Saint)	Lord Chancellor to Henry VIII	St Peter ad Vincula, Tower of London Head: Canterbury
Morland, George	Artist	St James's Church. Site occupied by Euston Station
Morland, Sir Samuel	Inventor and courtier	St Paul's Church, Queen Caroline Street (U Hammersmith)
Mulready, William	Artist	Kensal Green Cemetery
Murray, John	Publisher	Kensal Green Cemetery
Nelson, Admiral Lord Horatio	Naval commander	St Paul's Cathedral
Newton, Sir Isaac	Philosopher and mathematician	Westminster Abbey
Novello, Ivor	Composer	Golders Green Cemetery (U Golders Green: B 2)
Palmerston, Henry Temple, Viscount	Prime Minister	Westminster Abbey
Pankhurst, Emmeline	Suffragette	Brompton Cemetery (U Fulham Broadway: B 16, 30)

Parr, Thomas	Reputed to have lived for 152 years during 10 reigns	Westminster Abbey
Peabody, George	American philanthropist	1 Westminster Abbey 2 South Danvers, Mass
Pepys, Samuel	Diarist	St Olave's, Hart Street (U Tower Hill: B 9a)
Pitt, William, Earl of Chatham	Prime Minister	Westminster Abbey
Pitt, William, the Younger	Prime Minister at age of 24	Westminster Abbey
Pope, Alexander	Poet	St Mary's, Twickenham (Train Waterloo: B 27)
Purcell, Henry	Composer	Westminster Abbey
Raffles, Sir Thomas Stamford	Founder of Singapore	Hendon, London (U Hendon Central)
Rahere	Courtier to Henry I and founder of St Bartholomew's Hospital	St Bartholomew's Church, Smithfield (U Barbican)
Ralegh, Sir Walter	Explorer	St Margaret's Church, Westminster. Head: West Horsley, Surrey
Reynolds, Sir Joshua	Painter	St Paul's Cathedral
Richard, Duke of York	Brother of Edwad V, murdered in The Tower	Westminster Abbey
Richardson, Samuel	Novelist	St Bride's, Fleet Street (U Temple: B 6, 9, 11, 15)
Roberts, Frederick, 1st Earl	Soldier	St Paul's Cathedral
Ross, Sir John	Explorer	Kensal Green Cemetery
Rossetti, Christina	Poet	Highgate Cemetery
Rupert of the Rhine	Royalist general in Civil War	Westminster Abbey
Rutherford, Ernest	Physicist	Westminster Abbey
Scott, Sir George Gilbert	Architect	Westminster Abbey
Scott, John, Duke of Monmouth	Leader of Monmouth Rebellion 1685	St Peter ad Vincula, Tower of London
Sellers, Peter	Actor	Golders Green Crematorium (B 2)
Seymour, Edward, Duke of Somerset	Protector, uncle of Edward VI	St Peter ad Vincula, Tower of London
Sheridan, Richard Brinsley	Playwright	Westminster Abbey
Siddons, Sarah	Actress	St Mary's, Paddington Green (U Edgware Rd: B 6, 8, 16)
Sloane, Sir Hans	Collection became British Museum	Chelsea Old Church (U Sloane Sq: B 19, 22)
Soane, Sir John	Architect: rebuilt Bank of England	St Pancras Old Church (U King's Cross: B 214)
Spenser, Edmund	Poet	Westminster Abbey
Stephenson, Robert	Engineer, bridge builder	Westminster Abbey
Stubbs, George	Painter of animals	St Marylebone Old Church (destroyed)

Sullivan, Sir Arthur	Savoy Operas	St Paul's Cathedral
Tauber, Richard	Opera singer	Brompton Cemetery (U Fulham Broadway: B 16, 30)
Telford, Thomas	Engineer, Menai Bridge	Westminster Abbey
Tennyson, Alfred Lord	Poet	Westminster Abbey
Terry, Dame Ellen	Actress	St Paul's, Covent Garden (B 6, 15, 77)
Thackeray, William Makepeace	Author	Kensal Green Cemetery
Thompson, Francis	Poet	Kensal Green RC Cemetery (B 18)
Thorndyke, Dame Sybil	Actress	Westminster Abbey
Tompion, Thomas	Clockmaker	Westminster Abbey
Tree, Sir Herbert Beerbohm	Actor	St John's, Church Row, Hampstead (U Hampstead)
Trenchard, Hugh Montague, Viscount	Founder of Royal Air Force	Westminster Abbey
Trollope, Anthony	Author (earned £66,939-17/6 from his works)	Kensal Green Cemetery
Turner, Joseph	Artist	St Paul's Cathedral
Tussaud, Madame Marie	Waxworks	St Mary's, SW3 (U Sloane Sq: B 19, 22)
Vanbrugh, Sir John	Architect, Blenheim Palace	St Stephen, Walbrook, next to Mansion House
Van Dyke, Sir Anthony	Painter	Old St Paul's (destroyed)
Villiers, Barbara, Duchess of Cleveland	Mistress of Charles II	St Nicholas, Chiswick (B 17)
Villiers, George, Duke of Buckingham	Favourite of James I and Charles I	Westminster Abbey
Watts, Isaac	Hymn writer	Bunhill Fields
Wellington, Arthur Wellesley, Duke of	Soldier, Battle of Waterloo	St Paul's Cathedral
Wesley, Charles	Evangelist, brother of John	St Marylebone Old Church (destroyed)
Wesley, John	Founder of Methodism	City Road Chapel
Wesley, Samuel	Brother of John and Charles	Westminster Abbey
Wesley, Susannah	Mother of John	Bunhill Fields
Whistler, James Abbot McNeill	Painter	St Nicholas, Chiswick (B 27)
Whittington, Sir Richard	Lord Mayor of London	St Michael's, Paternoster Row (destroyed)
Wilberforce, William	MP; anti-slavery campaigner	Westminster Abbey
Wilkes, John	MP and editor	Grosvenor Chapel, South Audley Street (U Bond St: B 6, 8, 12 etc)
Wolfe, General James	Soldier, battle of Quebec	St Alfege Church, Greenwich (river bus, Westminster Pier)
Wood, Sir Henry	Conductor	St Sepulchre, Giltsput St (U St Paul's: B 8, 22, 25)

Wren, Sir Christopher	Architect, St Paul's Cathedral	St Paul's Cathedral
Wycherley, William	Dramatist	St Paul's, Covent Garden (B 6, 15, 77)

How to Get There

Bunhill Fields Cemetery, City Road (Underground: Old Street; Bus: 76).
Highgate Cemetery, Swains Lane (Bus: 210, 214, 271).
Kensal Green Cemetery (Underground: Kensal Green; Bus: 18, 52).
St Paul's Cathedral, Ludgate Circus (Underground: St Paul's; Bus: 6, 13, 60, 15).
Tower of London, Tower Hill (Underground: Tower Hill).
Westminster Abbey and St Margaret's Church (Underground: Westminster; Bus: 3, 11, 12, 24, 29, 53, 88, 159).

In other places U for Underground and B for Bus follows the location of the grave.

OUTSIDE LONDON

Arthur (and Guinevere)	Saxon king (and queen)	Glastonburgy Abbey (ruins)
Becket, Thomas	Saint/Archbishop of Canterbury	Winchester Cathedral
Boswell, James	Biographer of Dr Johnson	Auchinleck, Ayrshire, Scotland
Brontë, Ann	Novelist	Scarborough, Yorkshire
Brontë, Charlotte	Novelist	Haworth, Yorkshire
Brontë, Emily	Novelist	Haworth, Yorkshire
Burghley, William Cecil, Lord	Statesman, adviser to Elizabeth I	St Michael's, Stamford, Lincolnshire
Byron, Lord George	Poet	Hucknall, Torkard, Notts
Byng, Admiral John	Shot to 'encourage the others'	Southill, Bedfordshire
Carroll, Lewis (Charles Dodgson)	Author *Alice in Wonderland*	St Mary's Church, Guildford, Surrey
Churchill, John Spencer, 1st Duke of Marlborough	Soldier, Battle of Blenheim etc	1 Westminster Abbey 2 Blenheim Palace
Churchill, Sir Winston	Prime Minister and author	Bladon, nr Blenheim
Clive, Robert	One of the founders of the Indian Empire	Moreton Say, nr Shrewsbury, Shropshire
Delius, Frederick	Composer	Limpsfield, Surrey
Disraeli, Benjamin, Lord Beaconsfield	Prime Minister	Hughenden, Bucks
Doyle, Sir Arthur Conan	Creator of Sherlock Holmes	Minstead, Sussex
Eleanor of Provence	Wife of Henry III	Amesbury Convent, Wilts (destroyed)
Elgar, Edward	Composer	St Wulfstan's, Little Malvern, Worcestershire
Eliot, Thomas Sterns	Author and playwright	East Coker, Somerset
Gilbert, Sir William Schwenk	With Sir Arthur Sullivan, Savoy Operas	Stanmore, nr London
Gray, Thomas	Poet, 'Elergy Written in a Country Churchyard'	Stoke Poges, Bucks

Harte, Francis Bret	American author	Frimley, Surrey
Hastings, Warren	Governor General, India	Daylsford, nr Stow-in-the-Wold, Gloucestershire
Herrick, Robert	Poet	Dean Prior, Devon
Holst, Gustav	Composer	Chichester Cathedral, Sussex
Housman, Alfred E.	Poet	Ludlow, Shropshire
Howard, Lord, of Effingham	Lord High Admiral at time of Armada	Reigate Church, Surrey
Inge, William	Dean of St Paul's	Brightwell, Berkshire
Jerome, Jerome Klapka	Author, *Three Men in a Boat*	Ewelme, Oxon
Kneller, Sir Godfrey	Painter	Garden of his home, Whitton, Middlesex
Lamb, William, 2nd Viscount Melbourne	Prime Minister	Hatfield, Herts
Langton, Stephen	Archbishop of Canterbury	Canterbury Cathedral
Laud, William	Archbishop of Canterbury	1 All Hallow-by-the-Tower 2 St John's College, Oxford
Lilly, William	Astrologer	Walton-on-Thames, Surrey
Lind, Jenny	Singer	Great Malvern, Worcestershire
Lloyd George, David	Prime Minister	On riverside, Dwyford, Caernarvon, Wales
Macdonald, James Ramsay	Prime Minister	Spynie, nr Lossiemouth, Scotland
Margaret Tudor	Sister of Henry VIII, wife of James IV of Scotland	Carthusian Church, Perth, Scotland
Marlowe, Christopher	Playwright	Deptford, Kent
Maugham, Somerset	Author	King's School, Canterbury
Meredith, George	Author	Dorking, Surrey
Montgomery, Field Marshal Viscount of Alamein	World War II leader	Binsted, Hants
Mountbatten, Louis, Earl	Last Viceroy of India	Romsey Abbey
Neville, Richard	'The Kingmaker' during Wars of the Roses	Bisham Abbey (destroyed)
Nightingale, Florence	Nursing pioneer	East Wellow, Hampshire
North, Lord	Prime Minister during American War of Independence	Wroxton Abbey, Oxon
Parnell, Charles	Irish political leader	Glasnevin Cemetery, Dublin
Peel, Sir Robert	Prime Minister, originator of police force	Drayton Bassett, Staffordshire
Penn, William	Founder of Pennsylvania	Jourdans, Bucks
Rolls, Sir Charles Stewart	Engineer, Rolls-Royce	Gwent, Wales

Dylan Thomas Memorial, Westminster Abbey

Romney, George	Artist	Dalton, Lancashire
Rossetti, Dante Gabriel	Poet	Birchington, Kent
Royce, Sir Henry	Engineer, Rolls-Royce	Alwalton, Hampshire
Ruskin, John	Writer	Coniston, Cumbria
Scott, Walter	Author, *The Waverley Tales*	Dryburgh Abbey, Border Region, Scotland
Shakespeare, William	Playwright	Stratford-upon-Avon, Warwick
Shaw, George Bernard	Playwright	Ayot St Lawrence, Hertfordshire
Shelley, Mary Woolstonecraft	Writer, creator of Frankenstein	St Mary's, Bournemouth, Dorset
Smith, Adam	Economist	Canongate Yard, Edinburgh
Southey, Robert	Poet	Crossthwaite, Cumbria
Stanley, Sir Henry Morton	Journalist, found David Livingstone in Africa	Pirbright, Surrey
Stephenson, George	Railway builder	Holy Trinity, Chesterfield, Derbyshire
Stern, Laurence	Author, *Tristam Shandy*	Coxwold, North Yorkshire
Swift, Jonathan Dean	Author, *Gulliver's Travels*	St Patrick's Cathedral, Dublin
Swinburne, Algernon Charles	Poet	Bonchurch, Isle of Wight
Thomas, Dylan	Poet	Laugharne, Wales
Tizzard, Sir Henry	Scientist, radar	Oriel College, Oxford
Turpin, Dick	Highwayman	St George's, York
Wallace, Edgar	Author of mystery stories	Little Marlow, Bucks
Walpole, Sir Robert	First Prime Minister	Houghton, Norfolk
Walton, Izaak	*The Compleat Angler*	Winchester Cathedral
Watt, James	Improver of steam engine	Hansworth, Warwickshire
Wesley, Samuel	Father of Charles and John	Epworth, Lincolnshire
Wolsey, Cardinal Thomas	Adviser to Henry VIII	St Mary de Fratis, Leicester (destroyed)
Wordsworth, William	Poet	Grasmere, Cumbria
Yale, Elihu	University named after him	St Giles, Wrexham, Denbighshire
Yeats, William Butler	Poet	Drumcliffe, Sligo, Ireland

11

Houses with Notable Connections

LONDON W1

Asquith, Lord	1852–1928	Prime Minister	20 Cavendish Square
Baird, John Logie	1888–1946	Originator of TV	22 Frith Street
Banks, Sir Joseph	1743–1820	President of the Royal Society	32 Soho Square
Boswell, James	1740–1795	Biographer of Samuel Johnson	122 Great Portland Street
Boult, Sir Adrian	1889–1983	Musician, conductor	53 Welbeck Street
Browning, Elizabeth Barrett	1806–1861	Poet	50 Wimpole Street, also 99 Gloucester Place
Burgoyne, General	1722–1792	C-in-C British Forces in American Revolution	10 Hertford Street
Burke, Edmund	1729–1797	Parliamentarian	37 Gerrard Street
Burney, Fanny	1752–1840	Novelist, diarist	11 Bolton Street
Byron, Lord George Gordon	1788–1824	Poet	Albany Chambers, Piccadilly
Canaletto (Giovanni Antonio Canale)	1697–1768	Artist	41 Beak Street
Canning, George	1770–1827	Prime Minister	50 Berkeley Square
Clive, Lord	1725–1774	Clive of India	45 Berkeley Street
Collins, Wilkie	1824–1889	Author	65 Gloucester Place
Copley, John Singleton	1737–1815	Painter	12 Leicester Square
Disraeli, Benjamin, Lord Beaconsfield	1804–1881	Prime Minister	19 Curzon Street
Dryden, John	1631–1700	Poet, dramatist	43–4 Gerrard Street
Faraday, Michael	1791–1867	Researcher into electricity	48 Blandford Street
Fox, Charles James	1749–1806	Statesman	46 Clarges Street
Gibbon, Edward	1737–1794	Historian	7 Bentinck Street
Gladstone, William Ewart	1809–1898	Prime Minister	11 Carlton House Terrace
Gwynne, Nell	1631–1687	Mistress of Charles II	79 Pall Mall
Handel, George Frederick	1685–1759	Composer	25 Brook Street
Hazlitt, William	1778–1830	Essayist	6 Frith Street
Hogarth, William	1697–1764	Painter, engraver	30 Leicester Square (later Sablonière Hotel)
Hunter, John	1728–1793	Surgeon	31 Golden Square
Irving, Henry	1838–1905	Actor	15a Grafton Street
Kean, Edmund	1787–1833	Actor	12 Clarges Street
Lear, Edward	1812–1888	Humorous writer	30 Seymour Street

Lister, Lord	1827–1912	Founder of antiseptic surgery	12 Park Crescent
Lutyens, Sir Edwin Landseer	1869–1944	Architect	13 Mansfield Street
Lytton, Sir Edward Buliver	1803–1873	Author	12 Grosvenor Square
Marryat, Frederick	1792–1848	Author	3 Spanish Place
Marx, Karl	1818–1883	Political theorist, *Das Kapital*	28 Dean Street (Quo Vadis restaurant)
Maugham, William Somerset	1874–1965	Author	6 Chesterfield Street
Moore, Thomas	1779–1852	Poet	85 George Street
Mountbatten, Lord Louis	1900–1979	World War II hero, last Viceroy of India	Brook House, Upper Brook Street, Penthouse
Mozart, Wolfgang Amadeus	1756–1791	Composer	20 Frith Street *see also* SW1
Nelson, Admiral Lord Horatio	1758–1805	Hero of Trafalgar	103 New Bond Street
Newton, Sir Isaac	1642–1727	Scientist	87 Jermyn Street
Nightingale, Florence	1820–1910	Founder of modern nursing	10 South Street
Nollekens, Joseph	1737–1823	Sculptor	28 Dean Street (Quo Vadis restaurant)
Palmerston, Lord	1784–1865	Prime Minister	94 Piccadilly *see also* SW1
Pitt, William the Younger	1759–1806	Prime Minister	120 Baker Street
Reynolds, Sir Joshua	1723–1792	Artist	Site now Fanum House, Leicester Square
Roberts, Field Marshal Lord	1832–1914	Soldier	47 Portland Place
Rosebery, Lord	1847–1928	Prime Minister	20 Chandos Street
Rossetti, Dante Gabriel	1828–1882	Artist	110 Hallam Street *see also* SW3, WC1
Ruskin, John	1819–1900	Critic, writer	31 Park Street
Shaw, George Bernard	1856–1950	Playwright	29 Fitzroy Square
Shelley, Percy Bysshe	1792–1822	Poet	15 Poland Street *see also* WC1
Sheridan, Richard Brinsley	1751–1816	Playwright	14 Savile Row
Smith, F. E., Lord Birkenhead	1872–1930	Lawyer	32 Gosvenor Street
Talleyrand, Count Maurice de	1754–1838	Statesman	21 Hanover Square
Trollope, Anthony	1815–1882	Author	39 Montague Street
Turnbull, John	1756–1843	Painter	29 Leicester Square
Wellington, Duke of	1759–1852	Soldier	Apsley House, Piccadilly
Wesley, Charles	1703–1788	Methodist	1 Wheatley Street
Winant, John Gilbert	1889–1947	US Ambassador to GB	7 Aldford Street
Woolf, Virginia	1882–1941	Author	29 Fitzroy Square

W2

Barrie, Sir James	1860–1937	Author	100 Bayswater Road
Churchill, Lord Randolph	1849–1895	Father of Sir Winston	2 Connaught Place
Hill, Sir Rowland	1795–1879	Inventor of penny postage	1 Orme Square
Marconi, Gugliemo	1874–1937	Wireless pioneer	7 Hereford Road
Schreiner, Olive	1854–1920	Author	16 Portesa Place
Stephenson, Robert	1803–1859	Engineer	35 Gloucester Square

W6

Coleridge, Samuel Taylor	1772–1834	Poet	6 Addison Bridge Road
Ouida (Marie Louise de la Ramée)	1839–1908	Author	11 Ravenscourt Square

W8

Beerbohm, Sir Max	1872–1956	writer, caricaturist	57 Palace Gardens
Browning, Robert	1812–1899	Poet	22 De Vere Gardens
Campbell, Mrs Patrick	1865–1940	Actress	33 Kensington Square
Chesterton, Gilbert Keith	1874–1936	Author	32 Sheffield Terrace
Clementi, Mario	1752–1832	Father of the pianoforte	128 Kensington Church Street
James, Henry	1843–1916	Author	34 De Vere Gardens
Mill, John Stuart	1806–1873	Philosopher	18 Kensington Square
Millais, Sir John	1826–1896	Artist	2 Palace Gate
Thackeray, William Makepeace	1811–1863	Author	2 Palace Gardens, also 16 Young Street

W14

Elgar, Sir Edward	1857–1934	Musician	51 Avonmore Road
Jinnah, Mohammad Ali	1876–1948	Founder of Pakistan	Stayed at 35 Russell Road
Leighton, Lord Frederick	1830–1896	Artist	12 Holland Park Road (now museum)

SW1

Arnold, Matthew	1822–1888	Poet	2 Chester Square
Baldwin, Stanley	1867–1947	Prime Minister	93 Eaton Square
Balfour, Arthur James, 1st Earl	1845–1930	Prime Minister	4 Carlton Gardens
Bennett, Arnold	1867–1931	Author	75 Cadogan Square
Cecil, Edgar Algernon Robert, 1st Viscount	1864–1958	Creator of League of Nations	16 South Eaton Place

*10 Downing Street (*Woodmansterne Limited Watford*)*

Chopin, Frederic François	1809–1849	Pianist, composer	4 St James's Place
De Gaulle, Charles	1890–1970	Soldier, statesman	4 Carlton Gardens
Derby, 14th Earl	1799–1869	Prime Minister	10 St James's Square
Gainsborough, Sir Thomas	1727–1788	Artist	82 Pall Mall
Gladstone, William Ewart	1809–1898	Prime Minister	11 Carlton House Terrace, also 10 St James's Square
Manning, Cardinal	1805–1892	Churchman	22 Carlisle Place
Moore, George	1852–1933	Author	121 Ebury Street
Mozart, Wolfgang Amadeus	1756–1791	Composer	121 Ebury Street *see also* W1
Newton, Sir Isaac	1642–1727	Mathematician, philosopher	87 Jermyn Street
Palmerston, Lord	1784–1865	Prime Minister	4 Carlton Gardens *see also* W1
Peabody, George	1795–1869	Philanthropist	80 Eaton Square
Pitt, William, Earl of Chatham	1708–1778	Prime Minister	10 St James's Square
Russell, John, 1st Earl	1792–1878	Prime Minister	36 Chesham Place
Sloane, Sir Hans	1660–1753	President of the Royal Society	Kingsmead, King's Road
Walpole, Robert, 1st Earl of Oxford	1676–1745	Prime Minister	5 Arlington Street

Marlborough House

SW3

Austen, Jane	1775–1817	Author	23 Hans Place
Brunel, Isambard Kingdom	1806–1859	Engineer, bridge builder	98 Cheyne Walk
Carlyle, Thomas	1795–1881	Historian	24 Cheyne Row (formerly no 5) now Carlyle Museum
Eliot, George	1819–1880	Author	Died 4 Cheyne Walk
Hunt, James Henry Leigh	1784–1859	Critic, poet	22 Upper Cheyne Row
James, Henry	1843–1916	American author	21 Carlyle Mansions (Cheyne Walk) (died after award of Order of Merit)
Langtry, Lily	1853–1929	Actress – the Jersey Lily	21 Pont Street
Rossetti, Dante Gabriel	1828–1882	Artist	16 Cheyne Walk *see also* WC1, W1
Scott, Robert G. Falcon	1868–1912	Explorer	56 Oakley Street
Turner, Joseph	1775–1851	Artist	118 Cheyne Walk
Twain, Mark	1835–1910	Author	23 Tedworth Square
Whistler, James Abbot McNeill	1834–1903	Artist	96 Cheyne Walk
Wilde, Oscar	1854–1900	Author	34 Tite Street

SW4

Barry, Sir Charles	1795–1860	Architect	The Elms, Clapham Common

SW5

Allenby, Henry Edmund Hynham	1861–1936	Field Marshal	24 Wetherby Gardens
Lind, Jenny	1820–1887	Singer	189 Brompton Road

SW7

Baden-Powell, Robert, 1st Baron	1857–1941	Founder of the Boy Scouts	9 Hyde Park Gate
Borrow, George	1803–1881	Author	22 Hereford Square
Churchill, Sir Winston	1874–1965	Prime Minister	28 Hyde Park Gate
Epstein, Jacob	1880–1959	Sculptor	18 Hyde Park Gate
Gilbert, Sir William	1836–1911	The Savoy Operas	39 Harrington Gardens
Hoover, Herbert Clark	1874–1964	US President	39 Hyde Park Gate
Kennedy, John Fitzgerald	1917–1963	US President	14 Princes Gate
Law, Andrew Bonar	1858–1823	Prime Minister	24 Onslow Gardens

SW11

Wilberforce, William	1759–1833	Anti-slavery campaigner	111 Broomwood Road

SW15

Swinburne, Algernon Charles	1837–1909	Poet	11 Putney Hill

SW17

Hardy, Thomas	1840–1928	Author	172 Trinity Road

SW18

Eliot, George (Mary Ann Evans)	1819–1880	Author	31 Wimbledon Park Road
Lloyd George, David	1863–1945	Prime Minister	3 Routh Road, Wandsworth

NW1

Beatty, Admiral Lord David	1871–1936	Naval commander	Hanover Lodge
Cochrane, Admiral Thomas, Earl of Dundonald	1775–1860	Naval commander	Hanover Lodge
Cruickshank, George	1792–1878	Artist	263 Hampstead Road
Eliot, Thomas Stearns	1888–1965	Poet	9 Clarence Gardens
Wells, Herbert George	1866–1946	Author	13 Hanover Terrace
Williams, Ralph Vaughan	1872–1958	Composer	10 Hanover Terrace
Yeats, William Butler	1865–1939	Poet	23 Fitzroy Road *see also* WC1

NW3

Constable, John	1776–1837	Artist	40 Well Walk
Freud, Sigmund	1856–1930	Psychiatrist	20 Maresfield Gardens
Galsworthy, John	1867–1933	Author	Grove Lodge, Hampstead
Hood, Thomas	1799–1845	Poet	28 Finchley Road
Keats, John	1795–1821	Poet	Wentworth Place, Keats Grove (museum)
Lawrence, D. H. and his wife, Frieda	1885–1930	Author	1 Byron Villas, Vale of Heath
Macdonald, Ramsay	1866–1937	Prime Minister	9 Howitt Road
Romney, George	1734–1802	Artist	Hollybush Hill, Hampstead

Scott, George Gilbert	1811–1878	Architect	21 The Grove
Wood, Sir Henry	1869–1944	Musician	4 Elsworthy Road

NW5

Blair, Eric (George Orwell)	1903–1950	Author	50 Lawford Road

NW8

Alma-Tadema, Sir Lawrence	1886–1912	Artist	44 Grove End Road
Huxley, Thomas	1825–1895	Biologist	38 Marlborough Place
McCartney, Paul		Pop singer	7 Cavendish Terrace

N1

Chamberlain, Joseph	1836–1914	Politician	25 Highbury Place
Lamb, Charles	1775–1834	Essayist	64 Duncan Terrace
Lamb, Mary (sister)	1764–1847	Essayist	As above

Keats House

N16

Defoe, Daniel	1660–1731	Author	95 Stoke Newington Church Street

WC1

Adam, Robert	1728–1792	Architect	1–3 Adelphi Terrace
Darwin, Charles	1809–1882	Naturalist	16 Gower Street
Dickens, Charles	1812–1870	Author	48 Doughty Street (museum)
Disraeli, Benjamin, 1st Earl Beaconsfield	1804–1881	Prime Minister	22 Theobalds Road
Fielding, Henry	1707–1754	Magistrate, Bow Street Runners	19–20 Bow Street *see also* WC2
Poe, Edgar Allen	1809–1849	American writer	83 Southampton Row
Rossetti, Dante Gabriel	1828–1882	Artist	17 Red Lion Square, *see also* W1, SW3
Shelley, Percy Bysshe	1792–1822	Poet	119 Great Russell Street *see also* W1
Smith, Sydney	1771–1845	Clergyman, writer	14 Doughty Street
Strachey, Lytton	1880–1932	Writer	51 Gordon Square
Yeats, William Butler	1865–1939	Playwright, author	18 Woburn Place *see also* NW1

WC2

Fielding, Henry	1707–1754	Magistrate, Bow Street Runners	Old Magistrates House *see also* WC1
Franklin, Benjamin	1706–1790	Inventor	Lodged at 36 Craven Street
Garrick, David	1717–1779	Actor	27 Southampton Street
Hardy, Thomas	1840–1928	Author	8 Adelphi Terrace
Heine, Heinrich	1797–1856	Playwright	32 Craven Street
Kipling, Rudyard	1865–1936	Author	43 Villiers Street
Novello, David Ivor	1893–1951	Composer, playwright	11 The Aldwych
Pepys, Samuel	1633–1703	Diarist	12–14 Buckingham Street
Rowlandson, Thomas	1756–1827	Artist	16 John Adams Street

E1

Barnardo, Dr Thomas	1845–1905	Founder of children's homes	Site of Solent House, Ben Jonson Road
Cook, Captain James	1728–1779	Explorer	88 Mile End Road

E3

Mahatma Gandhi	1869–1948	Father of Indian independence	Kingsley Hall, Powis Road

Staple Inn

EC1

Barry, Sir Charles	1795–1860	Architect	39 Ely Place
Wesley, John	1703–1791	Evangelist	47 City Road

EC2

Hood, Thomas	1799–1845	Poet	31 Poultry

EC4

Goldsmith, Oliver	1728–1774	Writer	3 King's Bench Walk, *also* 6 Wine Office Court
Johnson, Samuel	1709–1784	Lexicographer	17 Gough Street

SE1

Bligh, Admiral William	1745–1817	Mutiny on the *Bounty*	100 Lambeth Road
Wallace, Edgar	1875–1932	Author	6 Tressillian Crescent, Deptford

SE10

Wolfe, General James	1727–1759	Hero of Quebec	Macartney House, Greenwich

SE24

Ruskin, John	1819–1900	Writer	26 Herne Hill

12

The River Thames

Throughout the centuries the River Thames has played a major role in the history of London. It is the longest river in England; about 120 miles (193km) direct from Lechlade in Gloucestershire to the Nore, or about 250 miles (402km) if allowance is made for the windings. The river is tidal from Teddington in Middlesex, and until recent years was an important waterway for commerce, with extensive dock and wharfage areas. These are now mostly closed for shipping, but are gradually being redeveloped for other uses – offices, flats etc.

There are many bridges over the river, with Tower Bridge perhaps the best known. The Bridge Museum and Walkway are open daily, but the bridge is raised once or twice a day to allow the passage of shipping. The times of raising are published on the back page of *The Times*. Stretches of the riverside are open for walks, eg the Victoria Embankment on the north, and the Albert Embankment on the south.

Perhaps the best way of seeing London is from one of the many pleasure steamers which go up and down the Thames all the year round. From Westminster Pier, Victoria Embankment, there are trips to many destinations such as Greenwich, Kew, Richmond, Hampton Court and the Tower, from which Greenwich can also be reached. It is advisable to check with the London Tourist Board Information Service, because some trips are subject to weather and tides.

Several interesting ships are permanently moored on the Thames. At Greenwich there are the *Cutty Sark* and *Gypsy Moth IV*. The *Cutty Sark* was launched in 1869 and was the fastest clipper afloat, covering as much as 360 miles (579km) on a good day. *Gypsy Moth* is the small boat which took Sir Francis Chichester on the solo round-the-world voyage in 1966–7. At Symon's Wharf, Vine Lane, near the Tower is moored HMS *Belfast*, the largest and most powerful cruiser ever built for the Royal Navy. It is now a naval museum.

One of the new Thames-side developments is St Katherine's Dock, near Tower Bridge, where 25 acres (10ha) of derelict warehouses, destroyed by bombs during the war, form one of the best of London's reclamation achievements. It now contains a marina, a pub – the Dicken's Inn – once an old warehouse, and the Maritime Trust's collection of old ships, including

A boat trip up the River Thames is not to be missed

The Cutty Sark

Discovery in which Captain Scott sailed to the Antarctic in 1901. London's latest tourist attraction on the Thames is the Flood Barrier, completed in 1983. This consists of a series of gates, stretching 570yd (521m) across Woolwich Reach, with main gates 67yd (61m) wide, raisable in 30 minutes.

13

Disasters

London's life has been affected by a number of disasters, starting with the Great Plague of 1665 and ending, hopefully, with the 'blitz' of World War II.

The Great Plague was a form of bubonic plague, which had devastated Europe for several hundred years, starting with the Black Death in the fourteenth century. In 1603 an outbreak accounted for more than 33,000 victims in London and, in 1625, there was another epidemic in which 41,000 died. After this, London was spared the plague for fifteen years until June 1665, when there was a worrying number of cases. These increased rapidly until September, when the onset of winter caused a decline in the disease, which lingered until 1666. About 69,000 people died in London, where the conditions were appalling. The doors of the sick were marked with a red cross, and the words 'May the Lord have mercy on us', and no one was allowed to enter or leave such premises. At first the dead were buried separately in coffins, but later they were merely thrown into pits. Many and varied were the remedies specified and sold by the so-called doctors, and fires were burned in the streets in the thought that they would stop the plague spreading.

The Great Fire is credited with the complete disappearance of the plague. It started on a Sunday in September 1666 and lasted four days and four nights, having broken out in the premises of one Farynor, the king's baker, in Pudding Lane near London Bridge. The houses in the lane, one of the narrowest in the City, had projecting storeys, and their woodwork was covered with pitch, so it was not surprising that the fire spread, particularly as there were no fire engines in those days. Farynor and his family escaped, but their maidservant did not, becoming the first victim of the fire. At first the flames spread slowly, but increased in volume when reaching the cellars and warehouses along the banks of the Thames, eventually setting London Bridge on fire. On Tuesday, Cheapside, Guildhall and St Paul's Cathedral were all destroyed. By Thursday 100,000 people were homeless, and all that had remained of Tudor London was gone. Casualties, however, were few, with not more than about a dozen fatalities.

The area of destruction within the City walls added up to 373 acres (151ha), with a further 63 acres (25ha) outside the walls. The list of casualties included 84 churches, 13,200 houses, 44 halls of Livery Companies, all the City gates, most of the Inner Temple, wharves, landing bays, all the markets except Leadenhall, all the gaols. The estimate of losses amounted to a value, of that period, of £10 million.

A happier outcome of the fire came with the rebuilding of the City under the guiding hand of Sir Christopher Wren. In addition to his masterpiece, St Paul's Cathedral, Wren designed 52 churches and 36 halls for Livery Companies, many of which survived the World War II Blitz, although a great many did not. Wren was also the architect for a number of other buildings outside the City, such as Chelsea Royal Hospital.

If the plague caused a large loss of life, and the fire a great destruction of buildings, the World War II Blitz took its toll on both life and property. It came after the Germans had lost the Battle of Britain in 1940, following which their High Command changed their tactics. London had suffered daylight raids previously, with relatively little damage, so the Germans decided to initiate night attacks. These were started in September, and continued until the following March. At their peak, in October 1940, the Luftwaffe dropped 9,000 tons of bombs on London but, although the damage was considerable, they lost 600 aircraft and the effective damage to the general war effort was not serious. Good dispersal helped industry, and rapid repair work meant that railways and the Port of London, a major target, were not out of action for long periods.

There was, however, considerable hardship and danger for the people of London, many of whom spent long nights in the refuge of tube stations or other shelters. No area escaped the bombing, though it was worse in the East End. It was estimated that 30,000 people were killed and 50,000 injured. Countless buildings were destroyed and streets obliterated; historic places such as Westminster Abbey, St Paul's and the Houses of Parliament were damaged, and the survival of St Paul's, amid so much destruction, must be counted as miraculous.

After the failure of the Blitz, Hitler launched an attack in 1944 with 'V' weapons, which caused a certain amount of loss of life and property, but came too late to have the effect for which they were designed. The V1 flying bombs were increasingly shot down, while the V2s, the heralds of the missile age, were unable to do too much damage before their sites were overrun. Even now, however, remains of buildings and sites bear witness to the devastation of the war.

14

Charles Dickens

One of the greatest, if not the greatest, of English novelists, Charles Dickens, is intimately connected with London where he first resided in 1814, though as he was only two at the time it probably made little impression. He was born at Portsmouth on 7 February 1812, and was baptised Charles John Huffam (after his godfather). His father, John, was a clerk in the Navy Pay Office, and his mother, née Elizabeth Barrow, was the sister of a fellow clerk. Before moving back to London in 1823, the family had lived at Chatham, then an important naval town.

They had not been in London long before his father, an improvident man – the model for Mr Micawber in Charles Dickens' semi-autobiographical novel *David Copperfield* – fell into debt and was confined to prison. He was at first in King's Bench Prison, Borough High Street, then was moved to Marshalsea in the same street. Little remains of Marshalsea, but there is a plaque on the remnants. A nearby public garden, alongside St George's Church, covers what was the church burial ground.

Charles went to work at Warren's blacking factory, at Hungerford Stairs, now occupied by the Victoria Gardens, Charing Cross. Some of his early experiences are recalled in *Little Dorrit*. While he was still at the factory it was moved to the corner of Bedford Street and Chandos Street, north of the Strand. From there he used to visit the White Swan tavern, now opposite the offices of J. M. Dent, who have published many of his works.

From the ages of twelve to fifteen, Dickens atttended school at the Wellington House Academy (now demolished) in Hampstead Road, from where he joined the legal firm of Ellis and Blackmore at 5 Holborn Court, Gray's Inn, renamed 1 Smith Square, in 1827. Later in that year the firm moved to 6 Raymond Buildings, which is still there. Having learned shorthand, he took a new job, in 1832, as a parliamentary reporter. The Houses of Parliament, as we know them today, did not exist then, and debates took place in Westminster Palace.

In 1833, his first literary attempt, a short story, was published in the *Monthly Magazine*. In the following year he adopted the pseudonym 'Boz', and gave up reporting for literature. The first monthly issues of *Pickwick Papers* appeared in 1836, and Dickens married Catherine Hogarth, daughter of George Hogarth, manager of the *Morning Chronicle*. It was not a happy marriage, because of incompatibility of temperament, and in 1858 they agreed to separate. But there was no stopping his career, and major works continued to appear with no signs of drying up.

Charles Dickens had many abodes in London. His first brief stay in 1814 was in Norfolk Street, Fitzroy Square, to which he was to return in later years. When the family moved from Chatham, they lodged at 16 Bayham Street, Camden Town, a site now occupied by a hospital, although some of the old houses remain in what was then a fairly rural area. The Dickens family had moved to 4 Gower Street (demolished in 1895) before the incarceration of Charles's father.

After his release, an acute shortage of money kept them on the move from lodgings to lodgings. There was a more settled stay at 10 Norfolk Street, Fitzroy Square (now 22 Cleveland Street), which still stands. So too does their next residence, 25 Fitzroy Street, next to the Yorkshire Grey public house. The family next went to 18 Bentinck Street, from where Charles used to walk to Lombard Street in the City, the home of his first love, Maria Beadnall, the origin of Dora in *David Copperfield*. Later Charles became tired of living with his creditor-hounded

Old Curiosity Shop (Woodmansterne Limited Watford)

parents, and took various lodgings, some of them in the Hampstead and Highgate district depicted in *David Copperfield.* In 1835 he was living at Furnivals Inn, High Holborn, first at No 13 and later, after his marriage, at No 15. This Inn of Court has now disappeared and the offices of the Prudential Insurance Company stand there.

After the birth of his first child, the family went to 48 Doughty Street, Bloomsbury, where Dickens wrote all of *Oliver Twist* and most of *Nicholas Nickleby*. This house was rescued from demolition in 1922 by the Dickens Society, and is now the headquarters of the Dickens Fellowship, and the main Dickens Museum, containing many relics, some of them from his American tours. It is open daily, except Sundays, and his time there is commemorated by a blue plaque. For a short time after the death of his sister-in-law Mary, to whom Charles was devoted, they stayed at Collins Farm, Hampstead Heath, and visited the public houses Jack's Straw's Castle and The Spaniards.

The arrival of two more children caused the move to more commodious premises, 1 Devonshire Terrace, York Gate, Regent's Park, where he was to remain for ten years. During this period he wrote *The Old Curiosity Shop*, *Barnaby Rudge*, *A Christmas Carol*, *Martin Chuzzlewit* and *David Copperfield*. This house was demolished in 1958 and the only memento of his stay is a bas relief, showing Charles Dickens and some of his characters, in the hall of an office block.

Little remains of the London which forms the background to some of these novels. There is an Old Curiosity Shop, but it is not that of Dickens; however the house from which Lord George Gordon addressed the Gordon rioters in *Barnaby Rudge* still stands in Welbeck Street, W1. The settings for *Martin Chuzzlewit* have mostly gone, but those for *Dombey and Son* have survived better. The blacking factory where Dickens worked, and the Wellington House Academy which he attended, are models for the Murdstone and Grinby warehouse and Salem School. There is a little statue in a small garden in New Kent Road in memory of David Copperfield.

The lease of Devonshire Terrace expired in 1851 and the family, now including six sons and two daughters, moved to Tavistock House, Tavistock Square, a building of eighteen rooms, demolished in 1900. Charles was to remain for nearly ten years, not a happy period because of his marriage problems. Among the works written during this time were *Bleak House*, *Hard Times* and *Little Dorrit*. Some of the background for these still exists, though Bleak House is not based on Tavistock House. The Inns of Court feature largely in the book, and Took's

Court, Cursitor Street near Lincoln's Inn, appears as Cook's Court. In Took's Court is an eighteenth-century house, named Dickens House; Tulkinghorn's house at 58 Lincoln's Inn Fields, where John Forster, Dickens' friend and biographer lived, still stands.

In 1855, Dickens bought Gadshill Place near Rochester in Kent and, in 1859, after the separation from his wife, sold Tavistock House and moved to this property. He was never again to live permanently in London though he kept an office at 26 Wellington Street, Strand, now demolished. He did stay for short periods in lodgings at various addresses in London, including 3 Hanover Terrace, NW1; 16 and 5 Hyde Park Gate, W2 and 6 Southwick Place, W2.

Of his later works, only *Our Mutual Friend* is largely concerned with London, particularly the river. One public house in Limehouse survives – The 6 Jolly Fellowship Porters is The Grapes, Narrow Street.

Charles Dickens died at Gadshill on 9 June 1870, and is buried in Poet's Corner, Westminster Abbey, having no monument by his own request.

15

Titles and Honours

PEERAGE

Princes and princesses are only of royal blood. Some of the princes have titles as royal dukes, ie Prince Philip, Duke of Edinburgh.

There are also non-royal dukes and they are followed in order of precedence by marquesses, earls, viscounts, barons, peeresses in their own right, life peers and life peeresses (barons and baronesses).

British titles are further complicated by the 'courtesy titles' which are granted to eldest sons of dukes, marquesses and earls. For example, the eldest son of the Duke of Bedford is the Marquess of Tavistock, while the eldest son of the Duke of Grafton is merely an earl.

The eldest sons of viscounts or barons have no distinctive titles and must make do with the prefix 'Honourable' before their names.

Most peers are entitled to seats in the House of Lords, as are the two archbishops – of Canterbury and York – and also twenty-four other bishops.

HONOURS AND ORDERS OF CHIVALRY

The premier order is the Order of the Garter, founded by Edward III in 1483. This is limited to twenty-four and is awarded by the sovereign to distinguished people. There are also, in addition, Royal Knights of the Garter, and some extra knighthoods awarded to foreign monarchs. There is a Scottish equivalent, the Order of the Thistle, limited to sixteen. They are followed by the Order of the Bath, which is divided into civil and (mostly) military divisions, awarded for service to the country. This order has three grades: Knight Grand Cross (GCB); Knight Commander (KCB), with the equivalent for women (DCB); and Companion (CB). Women became eligible in 1971.

The Order of Merit, which comes next, is awarded to eminent people, without conferring a knighthood. This is limited to twenty-four members.

The Order of St Michael and St George is awarded to

members of the Diplomatic Corps and, like the Bath, is in three grades: GCMG, KCMG or CMG. The Royal Victorian Order is awarded for personal service to the monarch and is, again, in three grades.

The Order of the British Empire is much the largest of the orders. It is awarded for services to Britain and the Commonwealth and is divided into five grades: Knight or Dame Grand Cross (GBE); Knight or Dame Commander (KBE or DBE); Commander (CBE); Officer (OBE); and Member (MBE).

There are, in addition, two other kinds of knight who do not belong to any order, but are also entitled to call themselves 'Sir'. These are baronets, an hereditary title, and knights bachelor, non-hereditary, the surviving representation of the ancient State Orders of Knighthood. The wives of all knights are called 'Lady'.

16

How to Trace Your Ancestors

1 Start from some factual point, such as Family Bible, letters etc.

2 Take all known data to the General Register Office at St Catherine's House, Kingsway, where they keep details of all births, marriages and deaths registered in England since 1837; or the Public Record Office at Chancery Lane for all information on Census returns from the nineteenth century.

For information before 1837, consult parish records and county record offices (assuming that information is available about which part of the country the persons in question came).

3 Several bodies can be consulted for assistance, such as:
Society of Genealogists, 37 Harrington Gardens, SW7
College of Arms or Heralds, Queen Victoria Street, EC4
Federation of Family History Societies, 96 Beaumont Street, Plymouth, PL2 3AC.
Mormon Genealogical Library, 64 Exhibition Road, SW7

The Association of Genealogists and Record Agents, 64 Oakleigh Park North, N20, will supply a list of about a hundred reputable researchers in Britain and, for those willing to pay from £150 to £300, Burke's Peerage, 1 Hay Mill, W1, will do high quality research.

Index

Page numbers in *italic* indicate illustrations.